PUT YOUR DEGREE TO WORK

PUT YOUR DEGREE

SECOND EDITION

W·W·NORTON & COMPANY

New York · London

TO WORK

The New Professional's Guide to Career Planning and Job Hunting

MARCIA R. FOX, Ph.D.

Published simultaneously in Canada by Penguin Books Canada Ltd.,
2801 John Street, Markham, Ontario L3R 1B4.
Printed in the United States of America.

The text of this book is composed in Times Roman,
with display type set in Benguiat Book Italic.
Composition and manufacturing by The Haddon Craftsmen, Inc.
Book design by Jacques Chazaud.

Library of Congress Cataloging in Publication Data
Fox, Marcia R.
    Put your degree to work : the new professional's guide to career
planning and job hunting / Marcia R. Fox. — 2nd ed.
        p.   cm.
    Includes index.
    1. Professions—Vocational guidance.   2. Job hunting.   I. Title.
HD8038.A1F69   1988
650.1′4—dc19   87–33771

ISBN 0-393-02580-2

ISBN 0-393-30550-3 PPK.

W. W. Norton & Company, Inc.
500 Fifth Avenue, New York, N.Y. 10110

W. W. Norton & Company Ltd.
37 Great Russell Street, London WC1B 3NU

1 2 3 4 5 6 7 8 9 0

For Leah and Lauren
And the memory of my father, Robert Fox

Contents

Introduction
to the Second Edition

When *Put Your Degree to Work* was first published in 1979, I was an assistant dean in charge of career development and placement at New York University's Graduate School of Public Administration. In that capacity my days were filled with counseling and placing job hunters of widely different backgrounds and distinctly individual needs. It was my conviction, as I wrote in the book then, that "Your education can equip you with certain training and skills necessary for professional success, but unless you are also skilled in the art of finding a job, you'll have a hard time entering 'the real world.' "

Nine years later the timeliness of that statement still pertains. Effective job search skills are at a premium because competition for jobs by college graduates has increased during the 1980s and will, according to the Bureau of Labor, increase markedly in the 1990s. Moreover, the challenge of career management in a society rampant with mergers, restructurings, downsizings, and other tumultuous forces means that workers need well-honed job search skills to survive and prosper over the long haul.

Much of what appeared in the first edition of this book still holds true today. Certain things about planning a well-organized job-hunting campaign will always hold true. I still believe—from my work with both employers and job hunters—that the burden of effort must rest with the job hunter. The person who makes use of career planning services and strategies during the undergraduate or graduate years, becomes familiar with the gearing-up strategies for a successful job hunt, knows how to prepare the kinds of résumé and letters that will attract an employer, and is prepared for that all-important interview is already many steps ahead.

This second edition adds extensive material on the logic, approach, and rationale of networking as the best job-search technique; informational interviewing strategies; and specific issues on the new job that ease the transition from student to professional. It reflects my own increased understanding of how job-search and career-development issues are intertwined. My own career change from academia to business undoubtedly fueled my thinking. In the course of designing and teaching courses on performance appraisal and career development to managers at Mobil Oil Corporation, I saw that many of the challenges faced by new graduates were also relevant for experienced workers, whose failure to grapple with "office politics," being a "team player," or other key challenges had significantly limited their advancement and/or satisfaction.

In my present job at Drake Beam Morin, Inc., a career consulting and outplacement firm that helps executives who have been terminated to find new jobs, I am project manager for Career Navigator ⓣ : The Computer-Powered Job Search System, a job-search tool for new professionals and recent graduates published during 1987. As a result, I have come to appreciate fully just how complex a task a job search actually is. Yet one's self-growth can be dramatic if it is understood that strategic planning, research, interviewing, communicating, time management, negotiating, and decision-making skills are all necessary skills.

It is my sincere hope that this updated and expanded edition will be useful not just in helping graduate-level students find appropriate full-time jobs and satisfying careers, but for undergraduates, for whom the advice is also applicable. In addition, the career changers or the women returning to the work place can also benefit, especially from the strategies for on-the-job success in chapter 6.

A proper acknowledgment of the contributors to this book would include the literally thousands of new professionals I have counseled and placed in positions over the years. Their questions, concerns, and successes enrich the pages of this book just as they have enriched my own perspective. Early on, colleagues at New York University gave me important encouragement in thinking that my ideas merited publication. My friends and colleagues at the Graduate School of Public Administration, Deans Dick Netzer and Ralph Kaminsky, provided me with an atmosphere of creative freedom to develop the career workshops on which much of the first edition of this book was based. Subsequently, colleagues at Drake Beam Morin, Inc., played an instrumental role in the creation of a new edition. I am particularly grateful to Bill Morin, Jim Cabrera, and Bob Marshall. Marilyn Machlowitz was as always a source of perception and sympathy. Carol Houck Smith, my editor at W. W. Norton, was committed and enthusiastic throughout. Finally, my mother, Leah, and my beloved daughter, Lauren, set an example of remarkable patience, support, and inspiring love.

November 1987   M. R. F.

PUT YOUR DEGREE
TO WORK

1

Career Management During Your Student Years

*T*o join that enviable elite of new graduates who seem to find the right jobs gracefully and easily, intelligent career management during your student years will be essential. If you make the most of these critical student years, you can acquire the requisite professional demeanor, skills, contacts, and practical experience that will help you to bridge the gap between the student and worker worlds. Employers want to hire professionals, not students, but professionalism cannot be learned overnight. It takes time and practice. And the best time to do this is while you are still in school.

This chapter shows you how to make the best of this seed

time. It emphasizes multiple actions that you, as a graduate or undergraduate student, can undertake to put into effect a shrewd career development program. You will discover how to exploit the often untapped career resources of your school. There is also a detailed guide to volunteer work and internships, the two kinds of practical experience most readily available. You will learn how to find these opportunities, where to find them, and how to use them to maximum career benefit.

Begin your career development program by discovering how you can introduce career considerations into your academic planning.

Academic Advisement for Your Future

Most schools have some system of required academic advisement whereby students meet with an assigned faculty member once a term to plan their curricula. Effective academic advisement should be a top priority, since the right courses with the right professors can get you off to a brilliant start and help you to emerge as a soundly trained professional. Too many students fall victim to a piecemeal or shortsighted approach to their curriculum planning for want of expert assistance. Returning women and career changers are in special need of good advice and may require more than one conference per term.

What can a skilled faculty adviser do for you? First of all, a faculty adviser with his or her feet on the ground can help you to come down to earth too. Curriculum planning, especially if you are in graduate school, should focus on the important relationship between your course of study and your career goals. If you don't know exactly what kind of job or career you eventually want, a good adviser can guide you toward a solid generalist education that will stand you in good stead, no matter what you decide upon later. To give such a general curriculum spice and marketability, your adviser probably can suggest an interesting minispecialty or guide you toward a cluster of marketable professional skills. Such skills can favorably impress employers when they appear later on your résumé.

Let's assume you do have well-defined career goals at the outset of your study; even so, your adviser may take a devil's advocate role and urge you toward a broad approach. This can protect you against the possible bankruptcy of dashed hopes or a later change of career direction. Your adviser will also challenge the kind of career anxiety that often leads to a premature or overly narrow specialization. You may need to have your eyes opened a bit.

When it comes to actually choosing your courses, a good adviser will have a comprehensive grasp of your field and will be able to point out important trends and dead-end specialties. A thorough knowledge of both school and university resources enables the adviser to suggest the most rewarding courses at your school as well as at other divisions of your larger university. He or she will help you achieve a proper balance between large survey courses and those smaller seminars where there is the opportunity for greater contact with faculty and for preparing research papers. Your adviser might encourage you, through remedial courses, to overcome a fear of mathematics or computers if these are important professional tools in your field. Finally, a good adviser will steer you away from poorly taught or lightweight courses or those that it might be preferable to audit.

If you are just entering a graduate program, obtain academic advice over the summer or well in advance of registering for your first semester or first year of courses. Even assuming that the bulk of your coursework consists of requirements, you may be able to take an elective.

If you are currently in the middle of a graduate program and already have an adviser, the following material should help you ascertain whether you have approached your advisement with the necessary care or have been treating it too casually. If you have been casual, you may wish to schedule a special appointment to mend your ways.

Finally, if you have been tolerating ineffectual or indifferent advice from a bored or uninformed faculty member, you should be turning informally to other professors or asking for a change of advisers through whatever appropriate formal mechanisms exist, such as the dean's office.

Effective advisement involves a partnership; it is essential that you take an active role. Even the most helpful or knowledgeable professor is not a mind reader. If you want specific suggestions tailor-made to your needs, you'll have to articulate your goals and concerns specifically. A vague question like, "Professor, what courses should I take?" will usually result in a vague answer.

The best-prepared student will motivate an adviser to give thoughtful and caring attention. Do your homework. Schedule your appointment well in advance of a busy registration period. Read about degree requirements and study course listings and familiarize yourself with the school catalogue beforehand. Prepare a list of questions about aspects of the curriculum that concern or confuse you. This is the time to find out what the school or university offers and how it applies to your own situation. For example, there may be eight possible sections of a demanding required course taught by eight different professors. Your adviser will be able to tell you which professor is most willing to devote individual time to his students. Or if you are uncertain which courses are the most pertinent for a future career in health planning, your adviser should have specific useful suggestions. Your adviser cannot necessarily answer all of your questions, particularly if they deal with specialty areas, but he should be able to suggest other avenues of help. It's also possible that you will be encouraged to see a career counselor.

Do not confuse the merit of the advice with the style of the giver. An extremely busy senior professor may seem intimidating and lofty; you may feel that he is inaccessible. However, his advice may be worth twice as much as that of the friendly but less experienced junior professor down the hall. The senior professor has a firm grasp of the curriculum and knows your school intimately. More important, he probably has the highly practical orientation typical of the distinguished academic with years of consulting experience. If you are enrolled in a professional school, nearly every faculty member will have extensive practical experience.

Even if your assigned faculty adviser is giving you excellent help, don't be timid about obtaining informal advice from other professors, especially those with expertise in specific areas that interest you. Asking the advice of professors with whom you have studied should be viewed as a natural and postive outgrowth of formal classroom contact.

Mapping out a thoughtful academic curriculum should be a measured and somewhat time-consuming task. If the process moves too quickly, your thinking may be superficial or glib. Considering options and seeking out informed advice should be an important developmental step. In planning your curriculum, you will probably also receive informal advice from your classmates. Listen carefully, but take suggestions and recommendations with a grain of salt. Even the best and brightest students can do little more than give you the inside scoop on exams and reading lists. And no student can help you take the long-range approach to curriculum planning that is ideal.

Here are some suggestions to help you emerge from your advisement sessions with a clear sense of direction and purpose. Not all of the suggestions may apply to you, but they should give you an idea of what you might reasonably ask.

1. If you are uncertain about your specific job interests, say so. Ask for help in planning a curriculum that will give you a solid generalist understanding of your field and help you prepare for the reality of a future job search. Your aim must be to develop a fail-safe and skill-oriented curriculum that will provide specific strengths as a bulwark against your uncertainty. Your adviser might suggest that you take two important survey courses, a skill-oriented course in an area like budgeting, accounting, statistics, or research, and a fourth course in a specialty area that intrigues you. Or your adviser may suggest an early practical exposure to your general career area—a workshop or a school-sponsored internship program. He or she may not have all of the specific answers to your career confusion, but your ability to articulate such confusion can be an important first step.

2. If you do have specific career goals, state them and test them out with your adviser. You might ask if they seem realistic for someone with your skills, training, and level of accomplishment. Even if your adviser thinks your goals are realistic, he or she may find them needlessly narrow or shortsighted and may urge you to broaden your career perspective.

3. In planning your curriculum, take full advantage of educational resources available from your university.

Courses taken in other divisions can enrich your professional perspective. For example, the aspiring business administrator would do well to take a course or two in public administration and vice-versa. A good adviser could probably suggest courses in other divisions. Or your own review of your university course offerings could generate questions and discussion.

4. If you are changing careers or are a returning woman worker, it may prove enlightening to map out a complete but tentative curriculum for your entire study. The very process of discussing courses with your adviser will help you to develop an awareness of the special vocabulary of your new career field. This vocabulary will become increasingly intelligible as you progress in your studies.

5. Discuss the value of gaining practical experience as an intern or volunteer. The proper timing of such experience will vary according to intern eligibility requirements and time constraints in your personal life, but your adviser may have some strong feelings on the topic that you would do well to hear. Your adviser can help you to choose between the volunteer and intern routes by summarizing the reactions of former interns: "My impression of the school internship program is that the application process is extremely competitive, but those who are accepted into the program find it a rewarding experience. Every student I have known has received a job offer from his or her internship supervisor. At the very least the internship is a good practical bet." An adviser may tell you about a little-known bulletin board where volunteer opportunities are frequently publicized.

6. If you are interested in obtaining research experience by working as an assistant to a professor who is on a grant or project, ask your faculty adviser how to go about finding such an opportunity.

7. Ask your adviser what kinds of competitive "academic" activities might be crucial, such as entering a writing competition for a school journal, competing for a prestigious summer internship program, or applying for a specific fellowship at your school. Your advisement session is the place to get early information about these activities since advance planning may be necessary. There are many students who do not compete for these awards or programs because they don't know about them or hear about them too late to apply.

8. If your school has a thesis option (or requirement), discuss it with your adviser early on. Specific recommendations for a topic or written guidelines could result.

9. Ask what else you should know about that will enrich your curriculum, prepare you for your intended career, and help you use your time wisely.

In summary, effective academic advice is an essential element in preparing to become a professional. Take full advantage of this resource at your school.

Career Counseling

Today most U.S. schools with an enrollment of more than 500 students have a full-time career counselor either affiliated with a placement office or performing the dual function of placement director and counselor. If your school does not have a career counselor, your central university placement or counseling center will.

As has previously been stressed, proper academic advisement, especially at the graduate level, must involve career considerations. However, there is a limit to the career counseling you can get from an academic adviser. You might ask your faculty adviser, "What art history courses are important for an aspiring museum administrator?" But you would visit your career counselor to ask, "How can I make myself more *marketable* as a museum administrator?"

It is not absolutely essential that your school career counselor have expertise in your particular career field, since a counselor functions as a generalist. A counselor may suggest specific career paths for someone with your talents and interests or may help you to weigh different career options and then refer you to others for advice. Once you have focused on a specific career direction, a career counselor may help you devise a job-hunting strategy, polish interviewing skills, or negotiate salary.

Despite a sophisticated awareness of the current "hot" specialties, a good career counselor does not have a crystal ball. Indeed he or she is likely to warn students in search of a sure-fire career path that today's hot specialty can be tomorrow's dead end. For a more accurate prediction of occupational trends, refer to the annual *Occupational Outlook Handbook,* a Department of Labor publication available in any good reference library. Or consult a computer guidance program that provides up-to-date occupational data, such as SIGI, available in most campus career centers or public libraries.

It is very important that you establish early and regular contact with a career counselor even if you are not yet looking for a job.

If you have just entered a program, schedule an appointment with a career counselor two or three months after the start of the term when you have had a chance to familiarize yourself with the school. If you are already midway through your degree, schedule an appointment as soon as possible.

Now let's turn to some of the basic questions you should discuss with a career counselor.

1. Ask about the current state of the job market for people with your specific goals, or—if your goals are still uncertain—for graduates with your specific degree. Find out how well recent graduates have done in the job market. Your object is to learn about their success so that you grasp which skills and specialties are currently in demand.

2. Ask the career counselor which professional skills will be most important to prospective employers. For example, a law student might concentrate on polishing research and writing skills. Now is the time to find out what skills you need to acquire or refine during graduate school. If you have already asked your academic adviser this question, no matter. Your object is to gain a head start on the process. The more information you can get, the better.

3. You might ask this question of your career counselor: "If you were just starting out as a student, what would you do to make sure that you prepared for your career properly?" The answer would probably include specific tips about your particular school. For example, the career counselor might say, "I'd make certain I got to know Professor Harris because she is brilliant, well-connected, and very helpful to students she knows and likes. I'd join the marketing club and take an active leadership role."

4. Ask if there are services devoted to résumé writing, interviewing skills, or career planning that your counselor can recommend. Some schools feature such workshops; others offer individual help. Still other schools maintain good career libraries or offer comprehensive computer job-search programs such as *Career Navigator* Ⓣ, published by Drake Beam Morin, Inc., in New York City, that will help you with self-assessment, skill training, the résumé, and other word-processing functions. Find out everything you can about the range and scope of career services at your school.

5. Find out about general and highly specialized professional organizations and associations that you should join. Do any of these have local or regional chapters? Perhaps the career counselor has application forms and publicity brochures relating to these organizations.

6. See if there are forthcoming programs, lectures, or meetings in your specific areas of interest. For example, if you are aiming toward management as a field, perhaps your counselor will know of a lecture by a management expert that is being sponsored by the American Management Association. Career counselors can be a mine of factual information and suggestions, but they may not think to volunteer them unless you ask for help.

7. Find out which student organizations are most active. Which contribute the most to the school?

8. If the counselor at your school also plays a placement role, you may want to ask about general placement procedures, or find out if there is a career and placement orientation provided for new students. An extensive discussion of how to use the resources of the placement office during an actual job search appears in chapter 2.

9. As with academic advisement, good career counseling requires your active involvement. Most of the questions earlier suggested for your academic advisement sessions could also be asked in a career counseling session.

The quality of any career counseling can be difficult to evaluate. After a session, consider whether the counselor made a genuine attempt to learn *your* needs and interests. If you have doubts, get a second opinion.

If the career counselor at your school also works in placement, this person could become a powerful advocate and resource in your eventual job search. For example, he or she might direct you toward actual job leads, refer you to useful new contacts, and generally give tactical and psychological support. Obviously it is in your best interest to build a positive relationship. Treat the counselor with the same courtesy, respect, and appreciation you would show a professor or a potential employer.

Now that you have benefited from thinking and talking about your career with others, it's time to consider independent activities that will contribute to your professional development.

Learning to Act Like a Professional

You can take concrete steps to start acting like a professional.

1. A good deal of your professional appeal will arise from an ability to *sound* like a comfortable and confident professional and to know insider terminology, since every group has its own language and slang. Begin to meet and talk with experienced professionals. Tap into

the "old-boy" network by attending cocktail parties, dinner programs, and lectures sponsored by local and regional chapters of key professional organizations in your field, such as the American Bar Association, the American Planning Association, and the American Society for Public Administration. Job interviews will be much easier for you if you actually engage in conversations with employers when the stakes are not as high (i.e. earlier on in your career).

2. Start reading the key professional journals and newsletters in your specific or general field of interest. You can find them in your university library. Cut out and file noteworthy items that might provide you with a lead to a summer job, alert you to innovators, or refer you to a reference publication useful in a job search.

3. Join one of the student clubs or associations at your school. Find out if there is a committee dealing with placement issues, professional development, or alumni relations. A placement committee may be involved in a research project with the school placement director; a professional development committee may organize a speakers seminar that brings prominent practitioners to the school; and the alumni relations committee may cosponsor workshops or panels where students can mix informally with alumni. These kinds of activities will introduce you to new people and help you to build personal relationships with administration or faculty serving as informal advisers to student organizations.

4. The annual conventions of professional associations in your field can offer you an early opportunity for professional exposure. The advance convention publicity that

is automatically mailed to members often asks people to suggest program topics, volunteer for panels, or present papers. Since students are a notable minority at conventions, the organizers feel a special responsibility to encourage student participation. If you prefer, offer your services to the conference chairperson as a general aide. You may get donkey work such as filing or typing, but the experience can give you a close-up look at prominent professionals.

5. If you have written an outstanding term paper, ask your professors to help get it published. An aspiring professional with a publication to his or her credit has a noteworthy credential. Or enter the manuscript in a student essay contest; these are often sponsored by professional associations and leagues, and the award may include both money and subsequent publication.

6. Compete for prestigious special intern programs or membership on an academic journal or review that publishes scholarly essays. These are the kind of honors that will help to build an impressive résumé.

7. Explore any special interests that are not covered by your curriculum through an independent reading course in which you obtain regular academic credit for independent study prearranged and approved by a professor. For example, an interest in juvenile justice may lead to extensive independent research, interviews with key people in the field, and perhaps even a subsequent stint at fieldwork. Developing such special interests can help you to discover important professional talents.

Professional Manners and Style

If you have never been employed as a professional, an understanding of professional "style" may elude you. To see just how much consciousness-raising will be necessary, you might want to evaluate your answers to the following quiz.

1. Have you ever handed in a paper late with a "personal problem" excuse? Yes_____ No_____

2. Have you often arrived for an appointment at school ten or fifteen minutes late? If so, have you immediately apologized? Yes_____ No_____

3. Are you usually at least five minutes late to class? Yes_____ No_____

4. When you wish to see a professor or an administrator, do you merely show up at his door? Yes_____ No_____

5. Do you turn in papers that have typographical or spelling errors? Yes_____ No_____

6. Do you often talk quietly in class to friends during a lecture? Yes_____ No_____

If you answered yes to any of the above questions, the chances are you need to sharpen your professional style. If you answered yes to more than three, others are probably perceiving you as unprofessional or immature.

You should be aware of attitudes that characterize professionals now so that they are second nature to you by the time you're ready for your job search.

Time Is Valuable

Time is money, so stop wasting yours and everyone else's. Even if your professors are relaxed about "drop-in" conferences, adopt a more professional style and schedule appointments with people you wish to see.

Punctuality is a related issue. Faculty members, administrators, or busy professionals may have rushed from a meeting elsewhere to meet with you in their offices. If your tardiness seems inevitable, call the appropriate secretary immediately to explain your delay and to find out if rescheduling is necessary. Do not show up twenty minutes late and expect to find your appointment still waiting for you or willing to give you more than a few minutes. It goes without saying that if you forget an appointment or cannot cancel in advance, always call or write a note of apology afterward.

Professionals Are Perfectionists

Many students manage to escape the adverse consequences of turning in sloppy or carelessly proofed work. Professors are known to be tolerant of mispellings and grammatical errors. However, the casual approach to details that is often the hallmark of the informal student style won't be acceptable forever. Once you are employed, sending out a letter under your signature that has two typos or mispellings will seriously undermine your image of competence. A grave error could even cost you your job, especially in fields where attention to detail is considered critical. One careless young accountant put an extra zero in a column, obligating his company to pay an extra $3 million.

Painstaking care with job-related application forms or required essays for competitive internship programs is also important. A selection committee will not be kindly disposed to an applicant who writes illegibly or turns in an ink-stained essay. One graduate student lost the opportunity for a coveted research position when an eminent professor decided to read the application essay in her graduate admissions file to determine her grammatical accuracy and neatness.

Finish papers and exams on time. Avoid taking incompletes in courses unless absolutely necessary. In your professional career, deadlines will be important; inability to meet them may damage your reputation and your relationship with colleagues. Get into the habit of taking deadlines seriously.

If the written word is not your strong point, start tackling the problem now. Once you are employed, grammatical mistakes or generally poor writing skills may be a handicap. Polish your writing skills in school, where tutorial help is readily available.

One hardly needs to be reminded that the most academically distinguished students usually have more choices at job-hunting time. If you are turning in less than your best effort academically, review the following truths:

Professors always exchange information about their best (or worst) students over lunch or during informal hallway conversations. Positive comments about you may lead to opportunities or job leads.

An outstanding performance academically will generally convince a prospective employer that you are a bright beginner. If you lack relevant work experience, looking like a bright beginner will be doubly important. Employers tend to view academic performance at this level as largely within your control. While an outstanding performance is interpreted as strong professional motivation, the reverse is equally true.

Ask for Help

Successful professionals are motivated adults who see themselves as responsible for their own destinies. They don't expect their bosses or other senior people to tell them or show them what must be done in order to advance. They learn to ask for help explicitly and judiciously.

Don't feel that it is an imposition to ask professors for letters of recommendation or specific career help. Professionals regularly ask for and receive favors from one another. They are generally extremely cooperative about offering copies of reports, access to events, lunchtime introductions, or help with on-the-job problems. Requests that might strike you as astonishingly self-serving are rather commonplace among people who know each other only slightly. They help each other in part because they expect the same courtesy in return.

So assert yourself to get needed help from your professors and school administrators. Not only will your action be perfectly appropriate but your professors will respect the motivation behind it, provided you are sufficiently courteous and appreciative.

You may feel, what with the staggering costs of school, that any help you receive from the school is due you. That doesn't alter the necessity for courtesy, especially if the helper has gone out of his way to make a special effort for you. It is always important to express appreciation and thanks, preferably in writing. This habit will stand you in good stead in the working world, where expressing thanks cements business relationships.

Keep Your Cool

Your response to frustrating situations during school is indicative of the way in which you will approach similar problem situations in the future. If you are quick to anger, learn to develop objectivity and control. There is little room for temper tantrums in the working world.

If you have a problem or complaint, always register it through proper channels. It is not professional to go over the head of a person about whom you have a serious complaint or to attempt to change a rule or system by bypassing the ostensible authorities. As a student, you should complain about a grade you consider unfair to the faculty member who gave you the grade rather than the person above him or her in the hierarchy. Similarly, any problem with a school rule concerning incompletes, registration, or other administrative matters should be taken up with the person in charge. If you feel that a "no" can be turned into a "yes" at a higher level, it is your right to appeal to the proper authority. In such a situation you could say, "I know that you don't have the authority to change the rule. But please tell me who might."

It is important to assert your rights and not be passive about procedures or events you consider unfair. But the way in which you assert yourself is crucial. For additional discussion of this important topic once you are employed, see chapter 6.

Building a Dossier

A dossier consists of professional work—term papers, publications—and any available work samples such as memos and reports. It is virtually anything that can illustrate the range and depth of your skills. At job-hunting time, a dossier can be a persuasive interview tool because it is a concrete example of your abilities. During graduate or undergraduate school, consider building a dossier by taking courses that require term papers and research projects. Another source of work samples will come from the substantive projects you tackle as a volunteer, intern, or paid employee.

The Importance of a Mentor

Considerable research attention has been given to the role of mentor in the development of a successful professional. Gail Sheehy's *Passages* (E.P. Dutton, 1978) and Daniel Levinson's *The Seasons of a Man's Life* (Alfred Knopf, 1978) both described the benefits of being guided up the ladders of professional success by a senior and more powerful advocate thoroughly familiar with company politics and eager to lobby on your behalf. Levinson defined the mentor's diverse roles as teacher, sponsor, host and guide, exemplar, counselor, and facilitator.

Some students are fortunate to find a mentor who helps them to accomplish the transition from student to professional. Although your adviser and a professor or two may take a kindly interest in your welfare, when they hear of a job opening they won't necessarily think of you. In contrast, when a mentor hears of a job opening, he'll think first of you and take the trouble to call you at home. A student with a mentor usually finds job hunting an easier task because a mentor enjoys facilitating the protégé's career entry.

Such personal commitment to your professional development is generally an outgrowth of a cordial working relationship. You may have taken several courses with a professor and visited him after class to talk about the field. Or you may have worked as his research assistant on a scholarly publication. The relationship will probably not spring up overnight, but rather will be an outgrowth of continued interaction based on classroom contact, research assistance, or school activities.

If there is a prospective mentor, seek out this person for your formal or informal adviser. Ask him or her for professional or academic advice, even if the person is a relative stranger. Asking people for advice can be the foundation of new relationships since most people enjoy the implied compliment the act represents.

The Value of a Contact Network

The importance of your contact network cannot be overstressed. Contacts will be your most fruitful source of leads and helpful advice at job-hunting time.

Earlier in this chapter, it was suggested that you attend conventions or institutes relevant to your field. Once there, you will undoubtedly observe the intense socializing that occurs among employed professionals. That cocktail-hour din is caused by the chatter of professionals busily keeping up their contacts with people who share specialized interests or similar jobs. Through informal gossip, professionals trade important and often privileged information.

Your classmates and professors are part of your current contact network. Make an effort to build strong relationships now for the years to come. For example, just as a fellow student may now tell you that a certain professor is looking for a new research assistant, at job-hunting time that same friend may identify an employer looking for someone.

Find out who are the influential people who may be in a position to give your career a substantial boost if they are acquainted with you. For example, if there is a professional you admire who has published widely, initiate contact by writing her a fan letter that also raises a substantive question. No matter how busy her schedule, either appreciation for the praise or professional courtesy will make her respond. Such initiative will help you to gain valuable confidence in your professional identity and provide a sense of adventure otherwise missing from most students.

Stay in touch with the people you meet. A Christmas card might be a good reminder of your presence, and a thank-you note is obligatory if you have received helpful advice. No one is too busy or too important not to be pleased at such flattering interest and attention. Any fear that you are "using" such people is completely unwarranted. Networking is a critical professional skill.

Fieldwork Experience during School

No good career development program for an aspiring professional is complete without practical exposure to the intended career field. Ideally, this might take the form of a part-time or summer job where you are paid for the privilege of acquiring experience that will make you more marketable. Unfortunately, such opportunities can be as hard to find or as competitive as permanent jobs. For the moment, we'll focus on the two possibilities that are easier to come by if you can clear your calendar for a minimum of three to fifteen weeks: volunteer work and internships. These are options that even the busiest of employed part-time students should consider, since the rewards are well worth the sacrifice of weekend or vacation hours.

It may be helpful at the outset to clear up the confusion among students, faculty, and employers about the exact definition of "intern" and the difference between an intern and a volunteer. Volunteer work is generally available to any enterprising person with or without an advanced degree. It is unpaid, and academic credit is not given. Traditionally, volunteer work has been considered the exclusive preserve of high school students (the candy striper) and women (the PTA). However, the kind of volunteer work we will be discussing is professional-level work that offers a challenge to both sexes.

An internship generally can be classified as one of three distinct types. First, there is the school-sponsored program awarding academic credit to students who complete a field-work assignment arranged with an outside organization. A detailed listing of the kinds of organizations that typically sponsor internship programs is provided in this chapter. Nearly all internship programs are administered by an intern coordinator who is either a faculty member or an administrator. The uniformity among internship programs ends with the coordinator. For example, some school internship programs pay a stipend; others do not. Some award letter grades; others award only pass/fail grades. Some are rigorous academic programs that require a substantive term paper; others impart academic rigor through a required series of seminars. For the purposes of this book, we'll be focusing on this kind of internship.

A second type of internship program is sponsored by a

nonuniversity group. Such programs may closely resemble job situations. For example, in the Summer Management Intern program sponsored by the New York City Urban Corps, approximately 100 undergraduate and graduate-level student finalists are placed as paid interns in selected city agencies. All interns attend required educational seminars.

The third kind of intern program is really a postgraduate traineeship. For example, the city of Phoenix sponsors a management intern program that is essentially a short-term job for people with recently acquired graduate degrees in public administration or business.

To add to the general confusion, there are many synonyms for an internship, such as "residency" or "practicum." The best way to evaluate a particular internship program is to look closely at its individual requirements.

Whether you embark upon a volunteer assignment or a school-run internship program, there are great advantages to be gained. Practical exposure to your field can make you look, act, and feel like the professional you hope to become. One important advantage is the early opportunity to test out whether your career direction is right for you. For example, an experience working as a consumer-rights advocate will enable a law student to get a feel for this specialty area and to practice important basic professional skills that have been limited to the classroom, such as drafting legislation or writing policy statements. Such work samples will probably be more impressive to potential employers than esoteric academic treatises. Another advantage of fieldwork is the potential exposure to professionals from whom one can learn. Their recommendations are apt to carry more weight with prospective employers than references from professors who have never seen you in a work setting. A substantive internship experience, if presented correctly on a résumé, can sound as impressive, if not more so, than any "actual" job. Moreover, during your job interviews, familiarity and ease with the special vocabulary used by professionals in your field can help to create rapport and convey the self-assurance of a proven professional. Fieldwork will test you, teach you new areas of strengths and interests, and allow you to profit from a beginner's mistakes. It's no wonder that many employers have great respect for such practical experience when they screen résumés.

Who best profits from such practical fieldwork experience? See if you can find yourself here among the people who generally find such experience rewarding and helpful:

- the graduate student with a recent B.A. who feels anxiety about finding the first professional job
- the determined woman returning to work who worries about the competition from younger classmates
- the career changer whose present direction is the result of a fizzled first career
- the unemployed recent graduate with an advanced degree who has little or no relevant experience
- the prospective graduate student who wants to take some time off before plunging into a graduate program straight from college
- the part-time graduate student whose full-time job restricts taking full advantage of the activities readily available to full-time students
- the undergraduate who wishes to determine a career direction or test out an early choice

For such people, practical experience generally provides a big boost in self-confidence and career direction. Moreover, the very task of finding and selecting the right fieldwork experience can involve many of the investigative, evaluative, interviewing, and negotiating skills so critical to a successful job hunt. Not only will volunteer work or an internship provide you with important practical skills but it will also help you to rehearse for job hunting.

Volunteer Work versus Internships

Current students with the option of enrolling in a school-sponsored internship program might find the ease of this more structured situation preferable to the greater independent effort and initiative generally necessary for a volunteer placement. Careful analysis of the relative merits of each alternative may help you to decide which experience best suits your needs. Keep in mind that some students do both. If that's your decision, choose a volunteer experience first and save the internship for a later time.

The following information may be pertinent to your decision.

1. A rewarding field placement is the essence of any fine internship experience. Unless your school can give you easy access to truly superior fieldwork opportunities, the experience you acquire in the process of locating a fine volunteer opportunity will be invaluable.

2. Internship programs require that students pay tuition fees. Consider whether it is worth it to you to spend a considerable amount of money to receive academic credit, especially if the internship program at your school does not pay a stipend to offset your expenses. Perhaps your tuition money could be better spent on a course that would teach you a practical skill, such as accounting.

3. Internship programs often include a special seminar series that will bring you into close contact with interesting guest lecturers in your field. This may turn out to be an important consideration. Find out in advance what you can about the seminar component of your school internship program.

4. Frequently internship programs require a substantial term paper or other academic component, whereas volunteer work rarely does. A term paper could turn out to be an important sample of your professional work to show potential employers. But you must consider whether you have the time and interest to supplement a work experience in this way.

5. One key to a successful field experience is the quality of the supervision you receive. The school intern coordinator should be able to steer you toward a supervisor with a proven commitment to the development of new professionals. As a volunteer, it may take substantially more effort to find a person willing to supervise you closely, let alone effectively.

6. Once you have obtained your placement and begun work, a school intern coordinator can help you with any initial problems. But there is a limit to the watchdog role schools can play. Schools cannot force an "unavailable" supervisor to turn into an interested mentor. And their sole recourse to exploitation or unfairness is to withdraw from future association. Whether you are an intern or a volunteer, you'll be very much on your own, and a successful experience will be largely your responsibility.

Look toward the future and ask yourself, "If I could have any job I wanted tomorrow, where would it be, and what would I be doing?" Your answer should be your starting point in exploring a volunteer or internship placement. For example, a goal as a psychiatric social worker with a family therapy specialization might lead you to an internship with a local psychiatric clinic that gives family therapy instruction to practicing social workers. Perhaps this clinic could use some extra help in coordinating or administering the instruction. Meanwhile you would have an opportunity to meet family therapists and observe clinical techniques.

The decision to aim for a job as a congressional staffer in Washington is another example. If you now live in Seattle, your best bet might be to begin working in your congressman's district office and hope that you could prove your worth there before trying for the Washington office later.

Or let's assume you aspire to be an editor for a publishing house. You might begin by contacting the relevant professional associations for editors, such as the American Book Publishers Council, to see if they sponsor a fieldwork program for aspiring editors. Professors who have published books may refer you to their editors for further helpful advice and leads. And one of them may be impressed enough to agree to sponsor you for a summer.

Always think in terms of working on projects, practicing *skills,* or getting *experience* in a specific career field. You should have something to do as well as to observe, because what you do can be put on a résumé. If, on the other hand, you can't answer the above question about a desired job, by all means see a career counselor on or off campus who will help you to assess your values, skills, and interests and arrive at an answer, however tentative. Or use a computer program to help you, such as Career Navigator ⓣ, Discover, or SIGI.

Now that you have focused on some ways to gain experience, it's time to transform theory into reality. Until you actually look for volunteer work, you cannot know whether you will be able to find your ideal setting or task. You may find something equally exciting in an entirely unexpected context, or you may have to revise your goals somewhat. The aspiring editor may end up polishing editorial skills at a magazine instead of in book publishing. Or the budding social worker might find that no local clinics provide family therapy instruction. However, she may discover an interesting group therapy fieldwork experience.

You begin to nail down your aspirations by thinking first of particular settings, specific projects, or possible supervisors. If you know a family therapist, for example, you would start with him/her. If not, you might start with a clinic. Let's begin with the volunteer, since volunteer opportunities are available to any interested person. At the same time, as we shall see, the volunteer route demands more initiative and imagination on your part than participation in a school internship program.

Volunteer Opportunities

Nonprofit organizations are typically the most eager for volunteers. The following list is intended as a sample of possible starting points.

senior citizen centers
community centers
church-affiliated special projects or grants
citizen groups such as block associations; police-citizen
    leagues like Citizens for a Better New York
nonprofit political organizations such as Common Cause

Mayor's Office of Volunteers
hospital volunteers organization
any religious philanthropy such as Catholic Charities
planning commissions
public agencies of any sort, such as budget offices
city council members
any ethnic or minority nonprofit service organization such
    as NAACP or Urban Corps
any health-related association, such as the National Coun-
    cil on Alcoholism, American Cancer Society
any consumer-oriented organization
any congressman or elected public official's district office
any community board
your own professional organizations, such as the student
    section of the American Bar Association, American So-
    ciety for Training & Development, etc.
United Way, Red Cross
federally funded special projects such as Cities in Schools
social fraternities or sororities for undergraduates, which
    often need alumni liaisons
museums, arts councils, art organizations
political campaigns
professional associations for various fields often sponsor
    internships
public affairs divisions of large, private-sector employers
task forces (usually announced in the newspaper)
chamber of commerce or associations of local business-
    people

This list is far from exhaustive. If you don't get the leads you
need from it, you can also consult:

The Yellow Pages of the telephone directory. Check under
a relevant "cue" word, such as engineer or energy; or use any

one of the following subject headings as a starting point: social service organizations; business and trade organizations; associations; political organizations; veterans' and military organizations; social settlements; clubs.

The Encyclopedia of Associations is a fine reference source available in any university or reference library and organized by specific field. For example, under the heading "librarian" are listed all of the important professional associations for librarians.

The card catalogue of a good library should also be checked for pertinent directories. Use the cue word of your field, such as "consumer affairs," or look up "internship" or "volunteer."

A mayor's office of volunteers will probably have a listing of volunteer placements available upon request.

Any university or graduate office that deals with students or jobs is apt to know of organizations looking for volunteers.

You might also get in touch with a specific person you would like to work with, like a prominent businessman who has volunteered time to a substantive civic project, a hard-working political appointee, or a public advocate.

Issues that stir your professional or personal enthusiasm are a likely source of volunteer work. You might, for example, feel disturbed at the plight of homeless citizens, concerned at the lack of employment programs for teen-agers, or dismayed by recent cutbacks in library services. If so, plan to join a group or organization tackling the specific project. (Or perhaps even start one.) Find out whether there are existing programs.

If there is an established program for volunteers (or interns), the next step is to find out the coordinator's name and obtain any required application forms. Be your most polite and professional self as you go through these steps, because the way you deal with people will probably influence how much they help you. If the organization you have selected does not have a specific program, forge ahead anyway. Even if they're not interested in students, they may get interested in you. Find out the name of the person in charge of the specific project or department that interests you, or the person who does the type of work that you want. A telephone inquiry ("Can you please tell me the name of the person in charge of ————?") will readily yield this information.

Next write an application letter to that person. A telephone call is less effective, since there is always the risk of an unwelcome interruption, and you may never get past a secretary or a receptionist. What's more, there is no written record of your interest. So write a letter first and then telephone.

Type the letter in standard business form. Make certain it is neat and free of spelling or typographical errors. At the top right put your address and a date. At the left put the complete name, title, company, and address of the person to whom you are writing. Make certain the letter is addressed to a *person* rather than a *function* (for example, Public Information Officer).

Mention how you came to write to this person and include a name if possible. For example, "Professor Harold Kelton recommended your office to me as a place that is deeply involved with the new————program." If you can't be that specific, the opening paragraph should always state your degree, current status (e.g., second-year student), university, and your desire to "intern" or contribute help. "Intern" is preferable to "volunteer"; employers seem to prefer this term.

In the next paragraph, give two or three details about your useful skills, your course concentration, or any related experience you think is pertinent. Make certain that you select these details on the basis of their likely appeal to the employer. Be as specific as possible. For example, "At Boston University, I have acquired skills in statistical analysis and research design."

State that you have time to contribute to a professional project on which they may need more staff assistance, and if possible, indicate the duration specifically, such as "From January through May, I have two days available weekly which I would be willing to commit to your organization."

Refer briefly to any prior experience as an intern or any other fact that would suggest that you are a responsible, mature person. Do not actually use these words to describe yourself. Refer to the résumé, which you should enclose, and, if possible, to a letter of recommendation. The latter will be particularly helpful if it attests to your maturity.

Ask for an interview at the employer's convenience. If you wish to be more assertive, state that you will telephone the following week "since I am rarely home during the day." The other alternative is to wait for a written reply. Most professionals will reply *eventually* to a written letter.

Close the letter by thanking the person for his or her time and signing "Yours truly." Type your name and write your signature. See also chapter 4, "The Cover Letter."

If you get to the interview stage, the rest should be relatively easy. Take with you an additional copy of your résumé plus any pertinent term papers or class projects.

You might prepare yourself by reading chapter 5, and plan to concentrate on the following:

Make it clear from the outset that your goal is to obtain professional-level experience. Of course you'll be willing to help out answering telephones if the office is occasionally short-staffed a few days, but your primary purpose is to work on a specific project, preferably a project they also care about. Their failure to commit themselves in advance may be a clue that they may intend to use you as a general "go-fer." If so, try to find another opportunity. (Your greatest bargaining power is *before* you start.)

Be forthright and specific about the skills you wish to polish or the projects that interest you. Don't put the burden of figuring out a "challenging" experience upon the interviewer. Nail down what you mean by "challenge" in advance.

Decide in advance exactly how much time you are willing to commit, lest you find yourself making a more significant commitment during the excitement of an interview. Establish a regular work schedule that you conscientiously maintain.

Before agreeing to a large-scale task, ask if it can easily be completed within the duration.

State clearly your desire to be supervised. If the project is substantive enough, this will follow naturally. You should *not* be free-floating.

Now that you've arranged a good volunteer placement, you may want to know more about internship.

The Internship

The school internship coordinator (generally a faculty member or an administrator) should give you invaluable assistance in finding a good placement, but both of you will have to bring intuition and judgment to the process. To allow the internship coordinator to do all the decision making while you sit by passively is like letting your parents dictate which graduate school you should attend. Take the time and effort to seek out the right placement for you.

1. Interview at more than one prospective placement so you can compare the merits of each.

2. Find out if any hiring has recently occurred at each placement. If your internship occurs during your last semester, aim for a placement where active hiring goes on. However, it would be both premature and presumptuous to mention your desire for "employment" during your interviews for the internship. (In fact, there is no reason to ask explicitly for a job. If these employers are interested in hiring you, no prompting will be necessary. And if they don't want to hire you, no amount of persuasion will help!)

3. Try to make some assessment of the amount and quality of the supervision you would receive. Good supervisors are generally busy and productive people who may want to test your motivation by asking you to submit a writing sample or to perform a brief project before agreeing to take you on. They are often as demanding in an exploratory interview as any employer. You might want to review chapter 5 before going on internship interviews.

4. Consider whether or not the assigned projects of the internship will help you to build basic and transferable skills in such areas as administration, grant writing, editing, physical design. Your goal at this point is to obtain practical experience and skills that have some degree of marketability.

Make the Most of Your Fieldwork Experience

There are no guarantees in life, but if you regard your field experience during graduate school as an apprenticeship for a permanent job, chances are you will be on your toes throughout. At the very least, aim to turn in your most outstanding performance. Even if your sponsor can't hire you, he is likely to recommend you to colleagues.

Here are some specific suggestions that should help you to get over the hurdles of inexperience.

ROLL WITH THE PUNCHES. Now that you have arrived at the internship, it's important to exhibit flexibility—the kind of flexibility that makes you offer to put aside your fascinating project and take over the office phones during a crisis. Don't expect everything to go smoothly at all times, especially in the beginning when you're very much a novice. Circumstances will settle down and you will settle down once you understand the routine.

No matter how brilliant you are, it's unlikely you will be handed a major or highly sensitive project until you have been tested on simpler tasks. If at the outset of your internship you are asked to perform a few clerical or routine duties, don't blanch. Expect to do them well and with a smile on your face. You are earning trust and respect. Your cooperation will pay off.

One way to get a job offer is to be an "eager beaver" intern. This may include volunteering to help someone else in the office besides your assigned supervisor. The more people you develop relationships with and the more projects you work on, the richer your experience will be. Having several advocates will also prove helpful at job-hunting time.

UNDERSTAND THE BOSS. According to management expert Peter Drucker, learning how to "manage" the boss should be one of the primary goals of any intelligent worker. Is your supervisor the kind of person who likes to read or hear a new idea? Find out quickly whether he minds frequent questioning or prefers prearranged information sessions. Creating rapport with the boss is a basic interpersonal task. Right now the reward may be a job offer. Later on the rewards may become even more significant, such as a major promotion.

ANALYZE THE POWER STRUCTURE. Keep a log in which you note down your initial impressions of the power structure of the organization. Since a newcomer cannot possibly figure this out right away, be on your best behavior with everyone, especially secretaries, who can have a good deal more information, influence, and general power than you might assume. At the end of the internship, reread those early notes. This is a valuable exercise. Whatever you have learned from your internship can be put to good use on your first permanent job.

At the end of each internship day, ask yourself what you have accomplished. If you have set daily goals, this task becomes even easier, because you can check them off. This is one way to make sure you are using this seed time productively.

ASK FOR FEEDBACK. You can obtain helpful and candid criticism from your internship experience. It can give you an important head start for your first job. But you may have to *ask* your supervisor for an assessment of you and your work. As a rule, most supervisors are unlikely to criticize an intern, because the intern cannot be held as accountable as an employee.

IF THERE ARE OTHER INTERNS. Like it or not, you will be compared with any other intern on the job at the same time. And the two of you may be played off against each other quite unwittingly, as when you are both given the same projects to assess. To avoid this kind of situation, take the initiative and get started on a project that interests you. Then you can show up the next day and say, "I was looking over the material on Poors, Inc., last night, and the thought occurred to me that they might be eligible for a. . . ."

Don't plan to compete with another intern. Concentrate on competing against yourself. That way you'll be spurred to your best performance.

BE CONSCIENTIOUS. This translates into simple good manners. Call when you will be late or absent, and inform the employer in advance if you expect to be absent for a school vacation. Take the internship as seriously as any paying job.

After Your Internship/Volunteer Experience

Ask your supervisor(s) if they would mind writing a letter to be used for general employment purposes. It should be addressed to "To Whom It May Concern." Ask them to discuss specifically the skills you demonstrated in executing various projects. Keep the original of the letter, make good reproductions, and plan to attach copies when you send out cover letters and résumés for jobs. Letters of recommendation are also useful for interviews, especially when you give the interviewer a copy of a relevant report on a project to which the letter refers.

KEEP WORK SAMPLES. Many graduating students keep work products or writing samples that can be produced on the spot for an interested employer. These samples allay the employer's anxiety about taking on a beginner who may have references only from a professor. The samples should be fairly short. Keep plenty of copies on hand.

ASK FOR ADVICE. The end of an internship is the ideal time for you to ask, "Where do I go from here?" See if you can get names of other professionals to talk to and ideas about ways you might best capitalize on what you have done. Reach out to the people who are in a position to help you get started on your career in a way that makes them feel good, helps you, and clearly establishes the professional role you will be playing in the future.

Never ask your supervisor for a job—at the beginning, middle, or end of the internship. You might want to mention that you'll soon be job hunting, but don't put the supervisor on the spot. A supervisor who wants to hire you will let you know without your asking. Let the employer take the initiative.

STAY IN TOUCH. After the internship is over, keep in touch with the professionals you've met. Write a brief note—perhaps on a Christmas card—or call now and then. Don't disappear for two years and then resurface with a request for job leads.

2

*The Effective
Job Hunt*

*T*he career counselor had met Dennis Himmel before at a fall alumni event. He had been a cheerful and forthright fellow then, but now in April he sat across from her in her office, barely able to mask panic and strain. She leaned forward and asked as encouragingly as possible, "Well, Dennis, what can I do for you?" He looked her straight in the eye with an urgency she had seen many times before. "How do I find a job?" he asked.

Dennis was like thousands of once self-confident students who suddenly crumble at the prospect of being expelled from the academic womb on graduation day without a job. A tight job market readily generates fear that one's degree will be an inadequate union card and that employers are capricious souls who hire according to arcane rules. Nearly every job hunter can point to a well-qualified friend whose painful struggle to find a job seems to illustrate how unfairly life can treat the worthy.

Fortunately, your job hunt need not put you into a state of panic. If you have read the preceding chapter, you are aware that careful preparation is the key to a successful job search. Now, with the immediate task of job hunting before you, there are other specific and consecutive actions that will give you a sense of control. Contrary to popular belief, there is nothing particularly complex or esoteric about an effective job campaign. It is a fairly clear-cut and logical process that can be learned by any motivated person who is good at getting along with people. The winning combination consists of advance planning; realistic and lucid goals; a properly timed job search; organized materials; and polished interview skills. It also includes using an existing resource, such as a placement service, in conjunction with the most effective independent job-hunting strategies.

Let's examine how an ideal job hunter goes about planning a job search, keeping in mind that the components of this search may have to be adapted to your unique needs. We might use Dennis Himmel as our example. Dennis begins by breaking down the task of finding a job into simple, manageable steps.

First he must focus his efforts so that he avoids floundering. Instead of asking, "How do I find a job?" he first asks, "What kind of job do I want?" Only when he has a goal can he stalk every clue and trace every lead with thoroughness and resourcefulness.

For example, if Dennis is a law student, he may already know that his goal is a job with a corporate law firm. If

Dennis is an undergraduate business student, he may know that he wants to enter the executive training program of a department store as a first step in a retailing career. If Dennis is an urban planner, he may hope to become an environmental planner with the Nassau-Suffolk Planning Commission in New York. If Dennis is obtaining a master's degree in political science, he may be somewhat less clear about his precise goal. He might aim for a job with a legislative official, or perhaps return to the employee benefits field where he worked prior to graduate school. Whatever Dennis's career field, it is imperative to clarify objectives and establish priorities among possible jobs. The results might sound something like this: "I would ideally like to be an environmental planner at the Nassau-Suffolk Planning Commission; my second choice is to be an environmental planner anywhere in the Northeast or in California; my third choice is to be a general junior urban planner in the Northeast; my fourth choice is to be a housing analyst, a career field where I have substantial experience and coursework."

If Dennis rejects this important clarification process by saying, "I'm not fussy. I am open to anything interesting," he is making it difficult for himself—a job campaign without specific goals is like a political campaign without a candidate. He'll need to clarify his thinking by obtaining career counseling.

Career counseling, which is becoming a standard campus service, will help you to:

- assess your values, interests, and needs
- identify your strengths by reviewing your accomplishments in previous jobs, volunteer work, or extracurricular activities and derive key patterns of skills from them
- use the preceding data about yourself to determine an appropriate job objective

If your placement office offers career counseling services, by all means avail yourself of them. Or ask for a referral to a *qualified* private practitioner.

Once you have developed a somewhat specific goal, the placement director's viewpoint can be invaluable, because daily interaction with employers gives the director a realistic perspective. For example, after Dennis has outlined his objectives, the placement director may tell him that the only place where the demand for environmental planners exceeds the supply is in the Midwest, not the Northeast. He may tell him that his second-choice job, urban planning, is relatively attainable and recommend attending a forthcoming Northeast regional convention sponsored by one of the many professional planning organizations. Or he may transmit welcome news that environmental planning is currently a "hot" planning specialty and that the Nassau-Suffolk Planning Commission has recently been recruiting junior planners. The placement director is in a position to save Dennis from false starts, futile efforts, and frustrating defeats. But he could not do so if Dennis merely asked vaguely, "How do I find a job?"

Dennis's next step is to establish a target employment date so that he can plan his campaign carefully during the next months. This is a crucial element. Once again, he will get advice from a placement director or another knowledgeable professional such as an urban planner. And he might say, "I am currently a first-year urban planning student. I expect to graduate in June of next year. I hope to be employed by July 1st at the latest. How far in advance should I begin my search for a job as an environmental planner? October or April? How far in advance are housing analysts hired? Is there a different lead time for a housing job search than for an environmental planning job search?" It is not Dennis's fault that he doesn't know when to begin looking for a job, but it would become his problem if he did not get expert assistance. He needs to know exactly when the hiring "season," if any, occurs. Also, the placement director can help him think through an overall strategy that takes advantage of his resources.

After this placement consultation, he buys a large calendar. Under specific dates he pencils in, "Start housing search," "Begin environmental search." Under July 1 he optimistically writes, "Start job today."

Dennis has already leaped ahead of most job hunters. He has already identified specific job goals, obtained realistic feedback from acknowledged experts, decided upon a target starting date for employment, and devised a time plan for accomplishing his job search. Having achieved such an efficient and productive start, he can now turn to getting his materials organized.

The first step is an effective résumé, the centerpiece of his job search (see chapter 3). Dennis's next task is to compose one or more sample cover letters to prospective employers. At the very least, he should familiarize himself with the components of a good cover letter, as outlined in chapter 4. Since a weak résumé and cover letter can seriously hinder a job campaign, getting an early expert assessment of these materials would be wise.

A reading of chapter 5, "The Interview," will be reinforced if Dennis can arrange to have a mock interview with a sympathetic friend, a professor, or even an employed fellow student. Dennis can learn a great deal about the art of interviewing from practice in articulating his goals, presenting his qualifications, and answering questions. The Interview chapter also contains many questions typically used by employers during job interviews. Two particularly helpful "tricky" questions are "Why should we hire you?" and "What is your major strength and what is your major weakness?" A mock interview should address itself to such questions and the possible answers.

The constructive criticism Dennis obtains from his mock employer, ideally a person with hiring experience, reinforces his strengths and helps him to recognize and deal with his weaknesses. Unfortunately, too many job hunters use actual interviews as warm-up experience. By then mistakes count heavily.

Dennis's last planning step is to seek the permission of his intended references. If their names will be recognized by potential employers, he may want to include them on his résumé; otherwise he will merely produce them upon request. It is basic professional courtesy to ask the permission of references in advance; it also enables Dennis to gauge their degree of enthusiasm about him.

Now that we have seen how the ideal job hunter plans a job campaign properly, let's turn to how you can structure specific elements of your job search.

How Your School Can Help You

Since the task of finding a job is an individual one, every job hunter should engage in independent and assertive efforts. However, this does not mean that you should not take full advantage of existing resources at your school that can speed you toward your goal.

For most aspiring job hunters, the school or campus placement office is one such primary resource. (Not every graduate school has its own placement office; many students must rely upon a central university placement service often staffed by a dozen people, each of whom performs a specialized task.

However, increasingly there are pressures upon graduate divisions with more than 500 enrolled students to offer specialized services in order to make graduates more competitive in a tight job market.) If your school does not have its own placement office, it may be in the process of setting one up or developing a faculty placement committee to supplement a central university placement office. Check with the dean of students to see what services may be in the offing.

The placement service perhaps of greatest benefit to job hunters is the sponsorship of the *on-campus recruitment program* whereby students are brought face to face with employers for campus interviews during fixed recruiting seasons. The jobs for which students interview generally do not start immediately but rather are part of a company or firm's major advance recruitment effort for this year's crop of the best and brightest. Not every placement office will necessarily sponsor such a program. Indeed only employers in selected fields such as law or business will traditionally hire months in advance of actual job openings. Otherwise there can be no recruitment program.

The processing of more immediate job openings is a more universal function that is accomplished through the placement office's *job referral system.* Here an employer who has a specific job opening notifies the placement office, which in turn notifies suitable applicants, either by posting notices on a bulletin board or by other systems such as a mailed newsletter or telephone referral.

The third function of a placement office is as an *information and career counseling resource* for job hunters engaged in independent efforts. Every placement office can and should fill this role, but many in fact do not due to insufficient staff.

Since proper use of an existing on-campus recruitment

program will require substantial advance planning on your part, let's turn to this placement function first.

The On-campus Recruitment Program

An on-campus recruitment program takes place in early autumn and often again in early spring. Its purpose is to bring together employers and well-qualified applicants who have indicated an interest in employment with them. The exact procedures for implementing a recruitment program vary widely from school to school. Generally, however, employers schedule one or two recruiting days at a placement office during a season that may be as brief as two weeks on some campuses and as long as three months at others.

Employers send along advance publicity materials such as a detailed letter (their "résumé"), annual reports, or recruiting brochures. The placement office sets up a library for these materials and other pertinent reference tools. In August or one month prior to the start of the autumn on-campus recruitment, the placement office distributes a recruitment schedule and detailed directions for obtaining interviews to all student participants. These sign-up procedures vary widely. For example, at some schools an interested applicant need only sign his name on an appointment schedule for a particular employer to be assured of an interview. At others, the résumés of interested applicants are prescreened by employers. At still other schools an elaborate computer program may match applicants and employers.

The kinds of employers who participate in on-campus recruitment represent organizations large enough to anticipate their hiring needs as far as eight months in advance and successful enough to be able to afford the considerable expense of recruitment. As a result, the on-campus recruitment program tends to reflect the "Establishment" rather than the smaller or newer employer. Some of the employers who interest you most may never participate.

If the recruiter is impressed by an applicant during the typical thirty-minute interview on campus, the applicant will be invited to participate in a longer interview at company headquarters. If the applicant survives this round of competition, he or she may receive a job offer as far as eight months prior to an anticipated employment starting date. Students who receive offers as a result of a recruitment program often have months to decide whether to accept them. Indeed some placement offices require participating employers to hold open their job offers until January 1 so that students can take full advantage of a long recruiting season without pressure to accept a job offer received early on.

For many students at law and business schools, on-campus recruitment constitutes the most effective and efficient way of finding a job. Even so, there are difficulties and disadvantages. One must be prepared for the often dehumanizing process of meeting perhaps thirty strangers across thirty desks in sterile cubicles at such inconvenient hours as 8:00 in the morning or 7:00 at night. Students and recruiters alike become exhausted at the intensive pace and extraordinary pressure to make a favorable impression in thirty minutes. Even the most charismatic and self-assured person finds it hard to project spontaneity into interviews with such rigid time constraints.

Unfortunately, large numbers of students are empty-handed after the interviewing marathon. This is not because they are unqualified; rather it is the direct result of the extraordinarily competitive nature of the process. For example, even the most superb interview may not lead to an invitation back to the company or firm unless the applicant has met fully the pre-established hiring criteria. Although such criteria are often spelled out in the recruitment materials sent to the placement office for students to read and review, there are equally important but hidden criteria. An applicant could not know that a specific company discriminates against applicants over the age of thirty. Another firm may "balance" its ethnic distribution by hiring Chinese applicants one year and Hispanics the next.

The competitive quality of the on-campus recruitment program is often difficult for the academically average student to grasp. He or she may feel it is worth a try to participate, and of course it is. But a wise applicant never depends solely upon this one route to a job, no matter how impressive his or her qualifications may be. And of course this would be especially true for the student whose grades are not outstanding.

Here are some suggestions that should make the on-campus recruitment experience more worthwhile for you. Let's assume that you are participating in an autumn recruitment program.

1. In June obtain a preliminary roster of employers who will be coming to your campus. If such a roster is not available, use the schedule for the previous year. Study the list to see if there are employers coming from cities that interest you, or from the type of companies or firms that appeal to you. Even the most cursory review of the recruitment literature sent by these employers will give you some idea of their special interests and the type of work available. Select twenty to forty employers. Then solicit the reaction of your faculty advisers, professors, and those senior classmates who have recently participated in an on-campus recruitment program. They

may be able to give you helpful information about particular employers on your list or suggest other worthwhile employers to add to it. Gathering advice is an essential step.

2. Schedule an appointment with the person who coordinates the recruitment program (the placement director or another staff person). This person generally has a great deal of knowledge about specific recruiters obtained through formal and informal contact. For example, during the recruiting season, the placement office often invites visiting recruiters to lunch; this public relations effort may indirectly benefit you when the lunchtime gossip turns to the recruiter's impressions of specific candidates interviewed that morning and the placement director reinforces a positive impression about you.

3. Ask for more information about prospective employers. You need to know which are realistic for *you*. You may learn that company X is an extremely hierarchical organization that prefers to hire only Ivy Leaguers for their training programs. Or you may be told that firm Y rarely extends a job offer to anyone who is not first or second in the class. This kind of discrimination may seem unfair, but a realistic preview will save you from building castles in the air.

4. Ask for suggestions about other employers that you might add to your list. The placement director may know of excellent training programs run by well-managed companies that you might otherwise have ignored.

5. Ask, "What else should I do to make the most of the on-campus recruitment program? What should I *not* do?"

Try to project professionalism in your conversation, for the recruitment coordinator may turn out to be a very powerful advocate.

The recruitment interview is a highly compressed experience. It is critical to project a self-confident and well-organized image. First, read and review chapter 5. Supplement this material, if possible, by talking with classmates who have been successful in obtaining several job offers through the recruitment program. They will undoubtedly have useful tips; one may even be willing to play a recruiter in a mock interview. If your placement office has a videotape of a recruitment interview, study it carefully.

You have only thirty minutes to make a positive impression on a presumably tired or bored recruiter. Your homework should include a thorough review of any available recruitment materials supplied by the employer plus a review of any other reference sources. These will enable you to develop a feel for the particular employer and work up some thoughtful interview questions about the company.

Decide which aspects of your training, background, or skills are relevant assets. You must have a very clear sense of what you want the employer to learn about you during the thirty minutes that will motivate him to invite you to a second interview.

Your résumé is apt to be an important tool at the outset of the recruitment interview, since a majority of employers will begin the interview by glancing at it and selecting an item to discuss. Thus it is important to highlight your most relevant assets at the beginning of the résumé, for it is un-likely the recruiter will notice credentials listed at the end. See chapter 3 for instructions.

Let the employer take the initiative at the beginning of the interview. However, if a monologue seems to be silencing you, you will have to break in gracefully. It is imperative to make the interview into a two-way conversation.

Follow up the interview with a brief but well-written thank-you note, and send it promptly. This can turn an employer's positive but indecisive impression into a second interview request.

If certain employers have prescreened your résumé unfavorably, it may be worthwhile to write to them directly for an interview at their headquarters. In many cases, well-qualified applicants have been screened out simply because the recruiter was limited to selecting only fifteen applicants from a group of several hundred résumés. Had that recruiter been interviewing a second day, you might have been selected. Moreover, by writing directly, you have the opportunity to include an effective cover letter.

If you are at a school where a computer matches applicants and employers and somehow you have been over-looked, you should definitely write directly to companies or firms that interest you. Your cover letter requesting an interview at their headquarters might say, "Unfortunately the computer has excluded me from your roster of inter-views. . . ."

What about Employers Who Can't Visit Your Campus?

Letters to those employers who solicit résumés from the placement office may yield off-campus interviews. There may be some system whereby the placement office collects and forwards résumés to the employer. Find out what the procedure is at your school. If possible, attach a cover letter to your résumé. The advantages of using a cover letter are outlined fully in chapter 4. It is worth reiterating that the on-campus recruiting program should only be one aspect of your overall job-search strategy. No matter how good your placement office is in securing employers to visit your campus, it is *unwise* to depend upon this process to the extent that most students do. On-campus recruitment is a grueling ordeal for many students. Unfortunately, some of the most deserving may not do as well as they should simply because they lack the steely nerves or personal charisma that the process often requires. As a safeguard, you must plan independently as well.

Now that you understand how to use an on-campus recruitment program to your best advantage, let's turn to the job referral function of the placement office.

The Placement Office Job-Referral Service

After you have obtained any necessary registration materials, schedule an appointment with the placement director or another staff member who works closely with employers. Your object in this meeting should be to understand how you can use a job referral service while you are exerting your own independent efforts. Here are some questions you might want to ask during such a meeting.

1. "I will be looking for a job as a _____ [your first, second, and third choices have already been established]. Does the office receive calls for such jobs?"

2. "Considering my goals and targeted starting date [also established earlier], how far in advance should I register with your office?"

3. "How are job leads processed? Please explain whatever system is used, and tell me what I can do to enhance my chances."

4. "If a job opening occurs that might interest me, how many other people from the school are likely to be competing for it?"

5. "When you receive job openings, are these openings exclusive to this placement office or are we in a competitive situation with other schools?"

6. "What else should I know that will help me?"

Let's assume you are now using the placement referral service and have completed all necessary registration forms. From here on, develop a good working relationship with the placement staff, who can take a special interest in seeing you happily employed. Fulfill your partnership obligations, whether they consist of replenishing your file with résumés, notifying the office when a lead has turned into an offer, or returning career library materials that you borrowed. Be polite and appreciative of any help you receive. If the office seems to generate a disappointing number of leads for you, it may mean that your expectations are unrealistic. Even the most effective placement director is not in control of the market. A wise course is to use the service to the fullest advantage possible, but never regard it as more than a supplement to your own independent efforts. Finally, keep the staff informed about the progress of your job search. Do not register with the office and then leave the rest up to them.

Now it's time to turn to your independent job campaign.

Your Independent Job Campaign

The independent job campaign requires major effort, so use your time and energy in the most efficient way possible. To do this, you'll go through a two-step process. The first includes early planning and information-gathering efforts; your placement office can be of valuable assistance here. During the second, you implement those specific strategies that have proven most successful for other aspiring professionals. In this chapter these strategies will be discussed in *descending* order of value. It's best to use a number of these strategies simultaneously, as early as three to six months in advance of your target employment date.

Early Efforts with Your Placement Office

During your independent job search, mine the resources of your placement director and office. Don't worry about becoming a nuisance. You are entitled to seek help repeatedly at this important time. The exploratory conference you now schedule with the placement director is no time to be passive or disorganized. Some of the questions you ask will arise naturally from your own unique needs and concerns. For example, you may be worried about your interview style and need specific coaching, or you may be confused about the proper timing of your efforts.

Other matters you should specifically ask about might include:

Specific postgraduate intern opportunities where you can get paid to learn. Your placement director probably has a file of these opportunities for interested students.

Placement office subscriptions to key professional journals or newspapers with a classified advertisement section that may be applicable to job-hunting students. Get recommendations for other journals to subscribe to or to read in the library.

Useful directories or reference tools, such as *The College Placement Annual,* in which recruiting employers spell out their hiring interests. Your placement office may have dozens of copies of this useful publication available as handouts, or may hide a single copy in a file drawer. No matter; a specific query will elicit the information.

A job bank subscribed to by your school or alumni directories available upon request to job-hunting students; some placement directors tap personal contacts for selected students as well.

Employer contacts who will give special treatment to any applicant personally recommended by a placement director, or employers constantly on the lookout for "interesting résumés." If you are fortunate, your placement director will share specific names and addresses or will forward your résumé directly.

Access to other placement services. Your placement director can contact other placement colleagues on your behalf at your university or an out-of-state university. You may get specific job leads through this route.

It should be obvious that developing excellent rapport with the placement director can motivate important efforts on your behalf. However, there are other early planning activities that you can do on your own:

If you are a graduate student who has been inactive in your *undergraduate alumni association,* renew contact with this potential source of job-hunting help. Many alumni associations or local chapters try to help job-hunting alumni by featuring a classifieds column in their alumni newspaper or setting up a placement committee. These efforts may be entirely separate from alumni placement efforts sponsored by a campus placement office.

Even if you have not yet received your graduate degree, you may be eligible to join *your graduate school alumni association* as a student member. Many alumni associations are so eager to build membership that they allow current students to join. If your future alumni association excludes student members, one of your school student associations or societies may cosponsor activities with alumni. Diligence in seeking out alumni contacts is likely to pay off.

Look for *special-interest groups and professional associations* with "talent banks" or "job banks" that bring job hunters to the attention of recruiting employers. For example, for the price of membership to the American Marketing Association, one can register with their personnel exchange. Such talent banks are worth exploring, especially since computerized features will likely permit employers to utilize them more fully.

Start reading and studying the *advertisements* in pertinent professional newsletters or publications. Develop an early feel for job terminology, new trends, and the kinds of employers likely to advertise in these publications.

Networking Interviews

Although it is a process often misused, little understood, and frequently disliked, networking—asking contacts for advice, information, and introductions—is undoubtedly the single best way to find a good job. Ask seasoned career professionals, corporate employment professionals, and career counselors, and in all likelihood they will agree that the conclusions of Peter Granovetter in his *Getting A Job: A Study of Contacts and Careers* (Harvard University Press, 1974) will still be true for you. When Granovetter studied the job search techniques of more than 10,000 professionals, he found that approximately 65 percent obtained their jobs through personal contacts. A surprising percentage were neither friends nor relatives but virtual strangers. Just as you are likely to find the best dentist or doctor in a new town by asking your contacts, so too employers prefer to hire people who come to them through the grapevine.

Let's look at why a contact network is such a powerful force on the employment scene. Believe it or not, employers are always looking for efficient and reliable ways to identify talented people. For them, placing an advertisement in a newspaper is as impersonal and tedious as it would be for you to seek out employers this way; employers prefer using the grapevine to screening on the basis of résumés alone. Typically they believe that the best candidates will be identified in "safe" ways—i.e., recommended by someone who can vouch for the candidates' honesty, stability, and trustworthiness. Evaluating a stranger carries risks, further complicated by the widespread falsification of résumés among job seekers.

Employers are strongly interested in meeting new people, even if there is no specific job opening at the moment. The process of networking and expanding their contacts is a familiar part of daily work life. And when they need to hire someone, they are likely to call upon possible candidates they have met or actively solicit names from colleagues. Indeed, when an employer needs to advertise or call upon an employment agency to fill a vacant position, it is usually because the networking system has flopped.

In addition, most like to be asked for advice. If the job

seeker is mindful of the employer's busy schedule and time pressures, most professionals enjoy being sought out and are willing to meet with you. It will of course be at their convenience, and you might have to wait or experience a postponement; however, chances are that you will gain an appointment with most of the people you approach.

Now let's look at this process from your point of view. During your job search, you will need to acquire information at each stage. For example, you will need to determine early whether your career goals are a good fit with your talents, identify the most appropriate target companies, and analyze key skills necessary for your chosen career. While research into books and magazines will help, interviewing others for information face-to-face will ensure the most individualized and specific information and advice. Such "information" interviews will also help you to plan a strategic job campaign, organize your efforts, and give you "inside information" about your field that will stand you in good stead later at job interviews. Perhaps equally important, those who take an interest in your candidacy are in a position to tell you about other people and opportunities, and provide tips not available elsewhere.

If the idea of deliberately seeking out advice, information, or introductions is a challenging and even intimidating proposition, don't worry; you are not alone. Practice will help, but networking is absolutely necessary whether you are a job seeker or an established professional of long standing, and it is important for you to cultivate this skill as early as possible. Make it easy for yourself by starting with people you already know and feel comfortable with (your primary contacts). They will lead you to others, people you may not know, but whose position or expertise may be more relevant to your needs (secondary contacts). Approached in the right way, meetings with these people to talk sincerely about your need for information can enhance your professional identity and maturity.

The experience may not be so intimidating if you realize that most people have enough nurturing instinct to enjoy talking with others entering their career field. During the information interview (in the course of having an interesting discussion), you might refer to a useful piece of research or a new book that would be of interest. You do have something to contribute to the conversation whether you realize it or not, and you need not worry that you are an "insignificant" job hunter asking for conversational alms. In brief, networking is best viewed as a two-way street where the persons you meet will also benefit.

Many people fail at networking because they misuse the process. They time their requests poorly (i.e., asking to meet with someone they have just met socially), or they use the information interview as a pretext (i.e., when they ask the person they are supposedly talking to about broader career issues or career facts if they are interested in hiring!). Networking is a subtle process that has its own rules.

In networking you are relying on your contacts for three things: information, advice, and—assuming that things are going well during the meeting—introductions to others. The one taboo is a direct request for a job. Ask only for things that others can easily give. People do not like to feel pressured about possible jobs, even if there are actual openings, when they have not really had the opportunity to evaluate you fully.

Be candid about the fact that you are job hunting, but be equally clear about only wanting advice or information from your contact. Indeed, use an approach with phrases like, "When Bill suggested I contact you, he didn't say that you were hiring right now, but he did highly recommend you as a person with great insight about career opportunities in our field." (Of course, the person could always say, "No, there are no jobs.")

Who are your contacts? They can include professors, friends, former employers, intern supervisors, administrators, former roommates, and professional acquaintances known to you already, plus anyone you might meet next week at a cocktail party or other social gathering. Like amoebas splitting, each contact can easily generate new contacts. During your job search, you should be constantly expanding your contact network.

Let's look at a few possible ways in which networking contacts can help:

The helpful professor. Sandra B was informed by her professor, a consultant to the Ford Foundation, that there was an immediate opening for a researcher on a large grant. She was given the name of the person directing the grant, who hired her on the strength of the professor's strong recommendation.

The accidental piece of information. Henry Brown happened to meet a classmate in a restaurant. During a casual conversation, he learned that his classmate, who had recently accepted a job, had just received an interview request letter from a company he had solicited several months before. He gave Henry the contact name. Henry followed up and got the job.

The access to useful strangers through family. Philip Eider was complaining about what a tough time he was having in the job market. His uncle offered to introduce him to his boss, who had excellent contacts in the engineering field. As a result of the meeting with the boss, Philip obtained the names of two new contacts who gave him helpful advice and one concrete lead.

The unexpected opening. Kathy Holzer was the hiring partner at a small law firm that had completed its hiring for the year by January 1. However, in February and March an unexpected increase in new business led to three new job openings. Kathy called three places for immediate help: her own law school placement office, an adjunct law professor friend, and her boyfriend's younger brother, a Yale law student. Within a week, her contacts produced fifteen résumés. She interviewed seven people and hired three. Had *you* been a job seeker the professor knew and wished to help, such inside gossip might have eventually landed you a job offer.

In each case, at the outset the job seeker could not have anticipated the outcome. What was essential was the process of talking with people about the need for help.

Here's how to adopt the contacts strategy to your own job search. First, list your contacts. The first few names will come readily to mind, but you may have to jog your memory for names from the past.

The professors at your current school who know you and who would recommend you without reservation.

Professors	Probably has good contacts in the field?	Thinks highly of you and would help	Knows you are looking now?
1. _____	_____	_____	_____
2. _____	_____	_____	_____
3. _____	_____	_____	_____

Deans and administrators at your school or university whom you know in any capacity.

Deans/ Administrators	Probably has good contacts in the field?	Thinks highly of you and would help	Knows you are looking now?
1. _____	_____	_____	_____
2. _____	_____	_____	_____
3. _____	_____	_____	_____

Every student in your current school or university with whom you regularly talk, eat lunch, or whom you simply respect. Your fellow students can be a major source of assistance, especially after they have found their own jobs.

Students	Is he/she currently job hunting?	Currently employed?	Knows you are looking for a job?
1. _____	_____	_____	_____
2. _____	_____	_____	_____
3. _____	_____	_____	_____

Contacts from any previous undergraduate experience: former professors, classmates, or administrators and deans; also any placement officials.

Names	Knows you are looking for employment?	Probably has good contacts?
1. _____	_____	_____
2. _____	_____	_____
3. _____	_____	_____

Contacts from internship situations and employers, colleagues, acquaintances who might remember you favorably.

Names	His/Her Career Field	Knows Other People	Knows you are looking for a job?
1. _____	_____	_____	_____
2. _____	_____	_____	_____
3. _____	_____	_____	_____

Personal friends, acquaintances, fellow churchgoers, or family friends who are either professionals or move in professional circles.

Friends, etc.	Probably has good contacts	Knows you are looking?
1. _____	_____	_____
2. _____	_____	_____
3. _____	_____	_____

Community organizations in which you have participated in the last five years—political organizations or campaigns, charitable organizations, and so on.

Organization and person	Probably has good contacts	Knows you are looking?
1. _____	_____	_____
2. _____	_____	_____
3. _____	_____	_____

Additional possible names including outstanding industry leaders who interest you but at this stage are unknown to you.

Names	Probably has good contacts	Knows you are looking?
1. _____	_____	_____
2. _____	_____	_____
3. _____	_____	_____

Family members, a frequently overlooked source. Even distant relatives may be able to suggest contacts.

Names	Probably has good contacts	Knows you are looking?
1. _____	_____	_____
2. _____	_____	_____
3. _____	_____	_____

The people listed above are generally all "primary" contacts—people you know already—who may lead to crucial "secondary" contacts, or people you don't yet know who might ultimately be more helpful than your primary contacts. A gym friend or neighbor might know a professional in your specific field who could be of special help. Yet unless you get that gym friend actively involved in your job search, it might never occur to her to introduce you to the professional. Since the random quality of networking is one of its most striking features, you cannot anticipate which person will lead you to a valuable outcome.

WHOM DO YOU APPROACH? How do you select among all the useful contacts you have just listed? Focus on clearly successful contacts who have demonstrated an interest in young people. Avoid seeking advice from people who are disgruntled, disappointed, or average at their jobs.

It's also important to understand that the advice you will get is only as good as the questions *you* ask. A man named John Smith was offered a job working for a dynamic managing director at a Wall Street brokerage house. In considering his decision, John Smith networked with Bill Bennett, an acquaintance who happened to work at the new firm, and asked for information about his prospective boss. "She's dynamic, brilliant, and electrifying," was Bill's answer. Had John been more shrewd, he would have asked more pointed, personalized, nuts-and-bolts questions such as: "What is she like to work for? Do subordinates have a chance to grow under her guidance?" Instead, John was swayed by Bill's generalized enthusiasm. He took the job, and only then discovered that the new boss was temperamental and quite aloof—an unpleasant combination.

CHOOSE THE APPROPRIATE RESOURCE FOR THE KIND OF INFORMATION YOU NEED. Select networking contacts based on the kind of information you need and then consider their comments carefully.

Use a disciplined, logical approach. First classify the type of information you need and only *then* identify the appropriate kind of person. For example:

Are you seeking feedback about yourself or your chosen path? If so, go to people who know you well enough to talk about what is right for *you,* or those who can at least talk soundly about your chosen career field, such as a person with broad experience and outstanding achievements. Be wary of seeking help about key decisions from strangers.

Do you need concrete career information about a particular company? If so, network your way to company "insiders" since they potentially have the most useful information. If you are lucky, they will give you candid and objective answers.

Do you need insight into an industry's future direction? If so, approach only a recognized industry expert. And get a "second opinion" while you are at it. You'll identify such experts from your own library research, faculty suggestions, etc.

HOW TO APPROACH PRIMARY CONTACTS. People you know well or see regularly (i.e., your primary contacts) can be approached directly, either in person or by phone. Typically, these people may not be in your intended career field, so your emphasis needs to be altered accordingly. You might introduce the subject in this way: "Since I am beginning a serious job campaign, I would appreciate a chance to ask you some questions and get some useful information (or advice) from you in a meeting at your convenience." If possible, during the meeting (*not* over the phone or in a few moments stolen during a social situation), outline your aspirations and seek information or advice that is tailored to your own needs. If your contact seems genuinely interested, you can then request introductions: "Can you suggest any employers who might be good for me to talk with?" Then, if names are suggested, follow up with, "How should I go about this? Should I call and use your name or write?" If your contact agrees to the use of his or her name, you are fortunate indeed, since such mention will probably ensure a "courtesy" interview with that new contact.

Of your three requests—for information, advice, or an introduction—the last is of course the hardest to come by. People won't be eager to have their names used unless they are sure you will represent them well. If it looks as though a contact is only willing to give you advice and information rather than specific introductions, don't push.

When you do have a name, here's how you might write a letter to that new person:

Mr. Gray Eminence
Investment Banking Firm
1 Wall Street
New York, N.Y. 10005

Dear Mr. Eminence:

Professor Jane Frye of the University of Southern California suggested that I write to you since you are a leading expert in the Urban Economics field. I have just received my B.A. in Economics from New York University and have studied and admired your recent book, *Smart Economics.*

I wonder if you might have a few minutes to talk with me about charting a successful career in urban economics.

Since my schedule is extremely flexible, I would be happy to meet with you at your convenience. I will call you next week to see if an appointment can be arranged.

Sincerely,

Mary Blackstove

When you approach a secondary contact "cold," without a name to smooth the way, a well-written letter is a graceful approach. Such a letter might read like this:

Dear Mr. Eminence:

   I will be receiving my M.B.A. in Finance from Stanford University's School of Business Administration in May. This semester I am deeply involved in an independent research project on Eurodollar trading procedures. In this context, I have repeatedly come across your name as an authority in the field. I have read, studied, and admired the article you recently wrote for *Fortune* magazine.

   I would very much appreciate an opportunity to talk with you briefly at your convenience about an investment banking career, since I have many questions and I am in need of expert advice.

   My schedule is extremely flexible and I can easily arrange to meet you at any point in your day that works best for you. I will call you next week to see if we can set up a date.

   Thank you in advance for your cooperation.

Sincerely yours,

William Rostick

   With a busy stranger, forging a link will be particularly important. You might mention a shared enthusiasm in a particular subject area, express your admiration for any pioneering efforts or special discoveries, or refer to his or her recent speech. You'll need all the cleverness and imagination you possess to forge that link.

   Wait one week from the time you send a letter and then follow up. Get right to the point that you are calling about your letter to him/her of October 25th so that you refresh the other person's memory.

APPROACHING A NEW CONTACT BY TELEPHONE. If you have good telephone skills, you may prefer to call rather than write. Try to call early in the week, in the early morning, and on a day when you can be at home to wait for responses, if a contact must return your call in order to set up an appointment. If you need to leave a message, say you are "calling at the suggestion of [Fran Smith]." If you cannot be there, an answering machine is essential since most strangers, be they employers or networking contacts, will not call back repeatedly.

When using the phone, what do you say? Be concise, to the point, and polite. State your name and the reason you are contacting this particular person (as opposed to someone else). For example, "You have the same kind of background that I do, but have made a big leap into a new field. I need to understand better how to marshall my own strengths." Ask for a brief meeting *at their convenience* and be prepared to be flexible.

Plan to call before 9:00 and after 5:00 if you hope to get beyond the protective barrier of a secretary. These are also the best times if your potential contacts answer their own phones. Here's an example of a telephone script to use as a guideline for your own situation:

"Mr. Smith, my name is Jane Adams. I'm a friend of Jill Sandler, whom I believe you know and who I hope told you I would be calling . . . (moment of discussion about Jill). As Jill told you, I'll be graduating next year from New York University's graduate business school with a major in marketing and have to decide which industry would be the best one for me to consider entering. I wonder if you might have a half-hour sometime in the near future to talk with me, since I'd really appreciate the opportunity to discuss some specific issues with you.

"You'll be going on vacation next week for three weeks? Oh, I see. Perhaps this is not a convenient time for you. Should I give you a call after you return in the middle of the week and then arrange a time?

"Fine, I'll put it on my calendar to call you on the 18th. In the meantime, have a good vacation. I'll look forward to meeting you when you return. Good-bye."

Notice Jane's politeness and easy acceptance of delay. Rather than pressuring Mr. Smith to see her, she quickly backed off when she learned he was about to leave for vacation. She also wisely took responsibility for initiating the next call, therefore giving herself more control and future likelihood of success than if she had waited for him to call.

AT THE INTERVIEW. First impressions count. So be on time, look professional, give the person a firm handshake, and smile during the introductions. And look the contact straight in the eye.

It is expected that you will get the meeting underway since you were the one who initiated it. After the initial pleasantries, say something like, "I really appreciate your willingness to talk with me today about some of my concerns. But before we get started, how much time do you have for our discussion?" If you know how much time you have, you can make sure that your most important questions will be answered.

During the interview, refer to prepared questions if you wish, but avoid taking detailed notes; it's important to keep eye contact. A smile or nod will indicate interest and create rapport. If the conversation seems to be slowing down, you can prompt more detail by asking a question such as, "That's very interesting. Tell me more about that." Needless to say, your interest should be sincere.

What happens if the person's conversational digressions threaten to stall your agenda? Gently try to get back on the track by saying, "That's very interesting, and it reminds me of an important question I haven't asked." Or, if it seems appropriate, use nonverbal signals, such as looking down or breaking eye contact for a moment. Such gestures could easily be considered rude if they are too abrupt, though, so be careful.

The conversation will be moved along not only by your own needs but also by the unique interests, personality, or orientation of your contact. Here are some guidelines to consider as you think about the ideal outcome of such a meeting.

Personal information. If you want to know how a person with your background and interests could fit into the field, you might ask the person to evaluate or comment about your résumé. The questions could be as specific as, "Where in the company (or field) do you think might be the greatest opportunity for someone with my interests and skills?"

Information about what it's like to be a professional. In this interview, you might ask broad questions such as, "During your career, what do you consider some of your most significant accomplishments? What were some of the most enjoyable experiences?" It is always fascinating to hear a successful person's evaluation of career success.

Information about the industry. Here you're searching for broad information about the field. You might ask, "Where do you think the opportunities are in this business?" "What do you think are the major challenges facing this industry in the future?" "What companies would you recommend as the best to work for?"

Information about a company. If you want to know about a specific company, you might ask an insider, "What's it like to work there?" "What does the company value?" "What are the career development benefits of working at this company?"

It goes without saying that before any information interview, you'll need to do homework, including developing an agenda and reviewing the company's annual report. When you walk into an interview, you should have a few well-thought-out questions.

Near the end of the interview you might ask, "Are there any important questions that you think I've left out?" If things have gone well, this is the time to bring up introductions: "Is there anyone else you can recommend I might also talk with?" Offer your résumé only if you are asked or if it can be done gracefully—i.e., so your contact can get in touch with you. If you have some sort of personal calling card, this is fine too. The issue of giving out your résumé is a tricky one, since it does not support your ostensible purpose for contacting the person. Giving out a résumé is the behavior of a job seeker, not someone interested in information. So be careful.

AFTER THE INTERVIEW. A prompt thank-you note is absolutely essential. While it need not be long, it should mention something you found of specific value during the meeting. Here is a possible sample:

Dear Ms. Sage,

    Thank you so much for taking the time to talk to me yesterday about a career in international banking. Bill Stefano had said that you knew the field thoroughly, but I never expected such an incisive review! I now feel very well prepared to make an intelligent choice of a first job.

    I am enclosing a copy of my résumé so that if you

hear of an appropriate opening, you can easily
contact me.
  Once again, many thanks for your valuable
advice. I'll keep you posted about my progress.

                              Sincerely,

                              Frank Conklin

Note that only after the meeting did the candidate present himself as a job seeker by enclosing a résumé.

It's a good idea to stay in touch with networking contacts. It's entirely appropriate, for example, to follow up an interview with a relevant article and a note saying, "I thought this might interest you." After all, you're building a network for your entire career, and it's important to keep the lines open.

Now that we have explored the most effective job-hunting strategies, let's move on to additional tactics. The first and probably the most likely to succeed is direct solicitation by mail.

Direct Solicitation by Mail

The employers you will be trying to interest through direct mail solicitation include those whom you *hope* will have a job opening (i.e., marketing letters) those whom you *know* have an opening (i.e., job application letters). Since all direct-mail solicitation involves presenting your professional credentials through a cover letter and a résumé, it pays to be a perfectionist about these materials; most of your competitors using a direct-mail technique will be sloppy, impersonal, or will avoid doing the necessary homework. For example, 300 letters addressed merely "To Whom It May Concern" will probably net three or four interviews. But fifty letters addressed to specific names will probably yield seven to ten responses. A thorough reading of chapter 4 on cover letters will certainly raise your consciousness about the employer's perspective in looking at both kinds of letters. It also outlines in detail how to write the kind of cover letter that will help you to sound and look like a professional. Similar guidance with regard to résumés appears in chapter 3. Your paper credentials must be impeccable in a direct-mail situation.

The Convention Placement Bureau

At the annual (and sometimes regional) meetings of professional organizations, such as the American Economics Association, the American Planning Association, or the Modern Language Association, a special convention placement bureau, often referred to as a "slave market", is set up for the convenience of employers with job openings and job seekers. During hiring booms, such placement bureaus at conventions take on importance; during retrenchment they become notably less effectual. Those job hunters interested in employment in the region where the convention is held or willing to relocate to jobs in "undesirable" areas generally do well, however.

If you are thinking of attending a particular convention for the sole purpose of finding a job, ask your professors to estimate your chance of success.

The dates of conventions are always set one year in advance. Annual conventions are generally held at the same time each year, with times varying widely from group to group. All members are told of convention dates, which are also available directly from the headquarters. If you are not a member of the professional organization in question, ask for a copy of any preliminary schedule or materials.

Here are some specific suggestions for making effective use of conventions:

1. If attendance will involve considerable travel expense, ask the placement director at your school to call the person in charge of the convention placement bureau about a week to ten days before the convention to find out if many job openings for junior professionals with your specific interests have been received. If you prefer, you can call the bureau directly. Explain that your investigative call is to help you decide whether to incur the expense of the convention. Do not write for such information; it is unlikely that you would get a reply.

2. Find out which of your professors are planning to attend the convention and ask them for help in advance. Give them copies of your résumé and stay in close touch with them during the convention. If several people from your school are planning to attend, perhaps there will be an organized effort to help job hunters by a faculty committee, representative, or even a placement director.

3. If you attend a convention for the specific purpose of job hunting, be an early bird. Bring a good supply of résumés, writing samples, and letters of introduction or recommendation. Plan to be at the placement bureau when the convention opens and *before* employers have been swamped with résumés or completely booked with interviews. Before your arrival, using a preliminary program, make up a list of the people you want to see. When you meet them, ask them if they know of anyone who is hiring.

4. Stay at the hotel where the convention headquarters are located so that interested employers can call you easily. There may be a message board system set up to reduce the number of telephone messages during the convention, but generally these message boards are little used. Be resourceful about reaching employers who interest you. Call their rooms or slip a note under the door. Take plain stationery with you so that you can attach a note to your résumé. Write legibly and put your hotel telephone number and room number prominently at the top of the page. State, "If no answer, please leave a message." Another alternative is to investigate if these employers will be appearing at a panel. If so, you can probably talk to them after the program.

5. It can be helpful to play an active role at the convention by arranging to be a panelist or volunteering to be a general helper at the placement bureau (either before or after your arrival). Avoid volunteering for activities at which you will encounter other students rather than potential contacts or employers.

6. The best place to meet people with similar interests is at the panels and programs. The best place for relaxed social mixing is at the cocktail parties or varied university receptions with a cash bar. Generally anyone can attend. Use both these opportunities for socializing with *strangers* rather than the familiar faces.

In summary, for the job hunter, conventions represent a working vacation where the informal contacts you make may prove more helpful in generating actual job leads than openings posted through a placement bureau. If you use your time intelligently, you can greatly increase your chances of finding employment via this route.

Job Fairs

The term "job fair" describes various kinds of one- or two-day recruitment events where employers interview interested applicants. Job fairs are often sponsored by university placement offices during late spring as a last-ditch effort to place job-seeking June graduates. Sometimes universities also sponsor a summer job fair or a minority job fair. The latter event generally occurs at schools in a nonurban or remote locale that recruiters are apt to overlook. Often an employment agency will sponsor a minority job fair, usually publicized widely in local newspapers.

Depending upon who is organizing them, job fairs can vary widely in their value to the job seeker. Since applicants rarely have to pay a fee, one has nothing to lose by attending. Probably the greater danger is in the unrealistic expectations such fairs often arouse.

Before spending money to travel to any non-university-sponsored job fair, find out the names of the companies attending and if they have specific job openings. If job fair applicants are required to preregister so that employers can prescreen them, it's a good sign. It means that employers are sincerely hoping to hire rather than merely compile affirmative action statistics.

The more information you can gather in advance, the more prepared you will be for scheduled or informal interviews. You will have had a chance to do useful research on firms or organizations and to prepare good questions. It would be a good idea to read chapter 5 on interviewing before you attend.

Finally, bring along extra copies of your résumé, work samples, and any strong letters of recommendation. Arrive early if you want to get maximum ease of access to employers.

Classified Advertisements in Newspapers

Newspaper classified advertisements are one of the most time-honored but *least* effective ways to get a job, especially for inexperienced new professionals. Two hours spent mixing at a cocktail party of your local professional organization is time far better spent than five hours responding to the classifieds on a Sunday.

Nevertheless, here are some suggestions for making this strategy more productive:

1. Find out the day when classifieds are printed and locate a newsstand that gets the paper at the earliest possible time. For example, the Sunday classified section of the New York *Times* is generally available days in advance. An early screening will give you a competitive edge.

2. Respond to classified ads with a résumé and a cover letter that have great visual appeal. Attach a strong letter of recommendation if you have one.

3. Be selective about the advertisements to which you respond, but don't be timid about applying for jobs that sound interesting but state requirements you cannot fulfill. The ideal applicant might bring two years of general business experience, but your internship and summer job experience might also carry enough weight. If the employer receives only a few responses or is not impressed by the responses he receives, he may want to interview you despite your shortcomings. Avoid ads that do not have the employer's name but only a box

number, since these are "blind" ads, notoriously useless. They are typically placed by employment agencies eager to collect bunches of résumés by writing about idealized but nonexistent vacant positions.

4. Provided the employer's name and address are given, your cover letter might say that you will call the employer's office on a specific day to see if an interview can be arranged. This tactic could move you into a "yes" category.

5. Do not expect employers to acknowledge your application. Under a deluge of responses, even the most courteous and sensitive employer is apt to forgo acknowledgement.

6. If you receive a response from the employer that promises to keep your résumé "active" or "on file," you have probably been relegated to the "round file." Don't expect to be called at a later date.

The Position-wanted Advertisement

If time has passed and you are now two months from your intended target date and still without a job, it might be a good idea to write a "position-wanted" advertisement. Insert your ad in a professional journal rather than in the classified section of a general newspaper, since employers most interested in people with your training are apt to advertise their job openings in the journal.

Be brief but comprehensive in your ad. Highlight your degrees, specific skills, and any pertinent information about geographical preferences or limitations. The last detail is especially important if the journal has a national readership to whom you wish to appeal. Keep in mind that this type of advertisement is most apt to attract employers who have had trouble filling their own job openings. The geographical location of the job or the noncompetitive salary may have deterred other applicants.

The style of the position-wanted ads in the journal you select can be used as a model for writing your own advertisement.

Employment Agencies

Employment agencies are not to be confused with executive recruiters or "headhunters." The latter deal with experienced personnel and are only occasionally willing to help an inexperienced junior person with extraordinarily impressive credentials.

Employment agencies are businesses that service employers who do not wish to take on the burden of finding the right employees themselves. The agency places the advertisement, conducts the job search, and refers selected applicants to the employer. When an applicant gets hired, the agency fee is paid by the employer.

Employment agencies can be extremely impersonal and mechanical in their approach to applicants. New professionals report feeling battered or bruised by the often graceless and hardboiled manner of the staff. To obtain the name of a good employment agency in your field, ask your school placement director or some experienced working professionals.

If and when you do get in touch with an employment agency, be sure you have a clear idea of the kind of job you want. Unlike career counselors, employment agency staffers have no personal interest in you. On any given business day, a hundred or more people may have come into their office from the street. Expect a no-nonsense approach that favors their clients' interests rather than yours.

Now that the independent campaign has been discussed, consider the particular problem of the job seeker not yet employed by his target date. Here are some suggested contingency strategies.

Working as a Volunteer While Looking for a Job

A volunteer stint during a job-hunting campaign can be a last-ditch way of making yourself more competitive. Detailed suggestions about finding volunteer opportunities can be found in chapter 1.

A volunteer may eventually be hired by the volunteer sponsor, so pick a volunteer placement where you would like a salaried job. Or choose one that is sufficiently prestigious to give an immediate boost to your résumé.

If you volunteer, make certain that you commit yourself to no more than a two-or three-day-per-week schedule for a fixed period of time. Do not overextend yourself. And do make provisions in advance for possible absences owing to job interviews.

Temporary Employment

If the wolf is at the door, part-time or temporary work is one way to pay your bills while continuing to look for the right first job. This stopgap effort may keep you from making the mistake of settling for a full-time job outside your field or a job for which you overqualify.

Short-term employment of this sort need not necessarily be added to your résumé. However, if after a year you are still working outside your field, it is important to supply some detail on your résumé. For example, one aspiring professional joined in her family's restaurant business when she could not get a job as a teacher. Two years later, when her parents sold their business and retired, she earnestly resumed a job search in her original career field. But the omission of the "irrelevant" two years on her résumé repeatedly aroused unnecessary suspicion among employers. Use your judgment in accounting for any time lapses.

What are some relatively fertile sources of part-time or temporary work? Retail sales, bartending, waitressing, babysitting, census taking, work as an office temporary, housecleaner, dog walker, personal secretary, night watchman, and bank clerk are only a few possibilities. These positions are readily found through employment agencies, Kelly Girl agencies, dormitory babysitting services, university student employment offices, or by reading classified ads in local or neighborhood newspapers. Ideally, try to get a temporary job in a company or industry where you'd eventually like more permanent employment if things work out. Call the personnel director at a specific company of interest and ask for the name of the temporary agency typically used to fill (clerical-level) jobs. Or, if you prefer, send the company a specific letter geared to a temporary but more professional-level position. For example, offer to do research, writing projects, or fill-in for someone on maternity leave. The idea is to position yourself well.

A Special Case: The Out-of-State Job Campaign

A good out-of-state job campaign requires substantially more time, effort, and expense than an in-state one. Proper planning requires that you target one or two specific places before you begin a serious campaign. The attitude, "I'll go anywhere" will probably get you nowhere, unless you are fortunate enough to have interviews lined up with companies that have regional branches. It is also extremely important to have well-defined job goals.

If you are a graduate student, the ideal time to begin your out-of-state search is while you are still a student. For example, a summer job in another state would enable you to put this experience on your résumé and make important contacts. Another alternative would be to transfer to a school in the desired geographical area.

If you are already seeking permanent employment, try to interview with any recruiters coming to your campus from the desired area. Even if these employers are not your ideal ones, a subsequent invitation to visit the company headquarters will give you a few days of useful time in the area. Otherwise your best bet is to solicit employers directly. There are many ways that you can get help at your school in developing a roster of potential employers. Ask faculty members and administrators to recommend alumni living in the new area or potential employers whose names they know because of consulting activities or other professional activities. There may also be an existing alumni chapter in the area or an alumni directory that you can use as a resource.

Start reading the local newspapers, preferably by subscribing to them. Your feeling for regional differences will become more sensitive, even if reading the classifieds may not be particularly fruitful.

Find out if there is a chapter of any pertinent professional associations in the new area or schools that may have a reciprocal agreement on placement services.

A telephone directory is a basic reference tool for discovering employers in your field. Find out, too, if the state publishes an official directory, often called a Red Book or Blue Book. This will be listed in the card catalogue of your university library under the name of the state. Scan the card-catalogue entry to see what other publications and reference tools might be available under "California."

Tell all your contacts of your desire to relocate. Actively solicit names of people living in the new area. Even if these new contacts are not in your professional field, they may be able to refer you to people who are.

In applying for jobs by mail solicitation, it is extremely important that your cover letter and résumé be carefully slanted toward the special requirements of an out-of-state job search. For example, emphasize in both your cover letter and résumé any prior connection you have had with the state in which you hope to relocate. If your spouse is from the state, you could mention this. If you are a native of the state or have lived there, add a "Place of Birth" entry to the personal data section of your résumé, allowing you to highlight this fact prominently.

Your cover letter must bait the hook by stating explicitly that you plan to be in California September 2–9 and would welcome an interview at that time. If you omit this important information, you'll probably get few responses. When supply exceeds demand, no employer is going to fly you long distance, especially if there is little in your background to suggest that your desire to relocate is anything more than a personal whim. Everyone, it seems, wants to go to Boston, San Francisco, Washington, D.C., the Northwest, and the Southwest. Employers in these areas receive thousands of letters per year, and one way to crack the barrier is by arranging to be in the area. If you get few nibbles, you can always cancel your plans.

The timing of your letters can also be critical. If the employer hires only on an "as needed" basis, no one time for an interview is preferable. If the employer recruits seasonally, send your letters well in advance of your competitors. For example, a law student would do well to aim for August interviews—the quiet before the recruiting storm. You can set up interviews for Thanksgiving or Christmas, but you risk the possibility that employers will have filled their vacancies by then.

If possible, get copies of any informational materials about your school, such as those likely to be used by a school placement office as publicity. You can either attach these to your initial solicitation or save them for the interview.

Collect letters of recommendation from professors who think highly of you. Attach the best letter to your cover letter and résumé if it is sufficiently specific and enthusiastic to do you some good. A letter from a professor with a national reputation would be most helpful.

Another possibility (which you can combine with the previously mentioned publicity brochure) is to send a one- or two-page excerpt of your writing. If nothing else, the enclosure should make you look serious about relocating. Be sure to send the entire package in a flat manila envelope. Do not stuff a legal-size envelope.

Finally, be prepared to undertake a big mailing. For every fifty or so letters you send out, you may only get two or three responses.

If all else fails, consider pulling up stakes and relocating even if you don't have a job. If you are that sincerely committed to relocation, you will probably manage to find employment once you are settled in the new area.

3

The Résumé

A résumé is effective if it gains you an interview. Most résumés fail to do this because they do not tell the employer what he or she needs to know—why you are interested in the job and what you can offer the organization—in a straightforward, focused, and visually inviting way. A résumé that incorporates your goals rather than merely sums up your past is the kind to write.

If you can arrange your skills and credentials in a pattern that the employer finds *relevant,* you'll be on your way toward looking like a professional (instead of an inexperienced graduate). Here are some of the advantages you'll reap: Your résumé will dramatically increase your interviews, actually predispose an employer to hire you, set the stage for interesting interview conversation, and serve as an effective postinterview reminder. In some cases, résumés have proved so appealing to employers that applicants were called in to interview for a previously nonexistent opening!

What are the distinguishing characteristics of a truly effective résumé?

1. It has visual appeal and is extremely inviting to read.

2. It highlights your strengths and makes the most of what you have to offer.

3. Its descriptions of your work experience emphasize problem-solving skills and specific accomplishments rather than mere duties.

4. As a professional document, it is entirely free of poor spelling, typographical errors, and trivia.

5. It provides all of the basic factual details that employers need and want.

6. It presents the most important and relevant information first and excludes or minimizes irrelevant experience.

7. It is succinct and organized in a loose outline format.

8. It does not exceed two pages.

9. It clarifies for the reader your professional direction either by being organized thematically or by including a well-stated job objective.

In this chapter, we'll deal first with those visual and mechanical aspects of the résumé that are not substantive but can nonetheless destroy the impact of even the most impressive set of credentials. Then we shall consider the heart of the matter: drafting a relevant and effective résumé. The last section covers such miscellaneous issues as how to handle details of salary, military service, and significant time lapses in your work experience. There is also a discussion of the résumé challenge to the returning working woman. The chapter is intended to be a comprehensive guide to résumés, eliminating the mystery and confusion new professionals often feel about this important and necessary document.

You might find out how much you already know about résumés by taking this brief true/false quiz.

Résumé Sophistication Quiz

1. A résumé must never exceed one page. True____ False____
2. Employers generally read entire résumés. True____ False____
3. It is not imperative to list a telephone number. True____ False____
4. New professionals should not be too specific about their career interests lest their résumé lock them into a specialty. True____ False____
5. School activities, internships, and volunteer work are of minimal importance to employers. True____ False____
6. Inexperienced job hunters should list their course work and/or attach a transcript. True____ False____
7. It is helpful to list a reason for leaving each job. True____ False____
8. It is perfectly acceptable to use "I" throughout your résumé. True____ False____
9. Employers are concerned about dates and often check for any time gaps. True____ False____

10. You must list all coursework taken at schools from which no degree was granted and all employment, however trivial. True_____ False_____

All the above answers are false. In the following pages each issue will be addressed in detail, but here is a brief review of the answers.

1. Try to limit your résumé to one page, but *never* do so if it means cutting short your accomplishments. A résumé of two pages is less preferred but perfectly acceptable.

2. Employers generally skim résumés and may only read the first few entries. Thus it is important to put the most relevant data at the beginning of your résumé.

3. It is very important to list a telephone number where a message can be left. Prospective employers are not likely to call you more than once or twice, and few will write you letters. They are most likely to call the next candidate. By all means purchase an answering machine.

4. It is not true that résumés should be general. Most résumés that fail are too bland and unspecific.

5. While employers would rather read about substantive jobs than an internship, if the latter is your sole experience, then emphasize it. You *can* make an employer sit up and take notice by highlighting both the results and skills.

6. Do not list all your courses on a résumé; this will result in more detail than the employer needs or wants. Use a "course concentration" as explained on p. 000. In some graduate schools, every job hunter who participates in on-campus recruitment attaches a transcript. If

this is the practice at your school or in your field, you should do it too. Otherwise the employer may assume that you are trying to conceal some aspect of your experience or lack of experience.

7. It is not helpful to list reasons unless you feel that a series of rapid job changes will make you look unstable.

8. Do not use "I" more than once or twice in your résumé.

9. Employers generally are not as concerned with dates as most job hunters believe. Avoid the common error of having the résumé feature dates more prominently or take up more space than other more essential information. Not until an employer is seriously interested in an applicant will he pore over a résumé checking for time gaps—and perhaps not even then.

10. With regard to all those summer school courses or minor part-time jobs as a camp counselor and library clerk, eliminate irrelevancies wherever possible, or else summarize the information *after* you have listed more important items. No one wants to know the street address of organizations you worked for in high school. If employers are interested, they can always ask for more information at interview time. The purpose of a résumé is not to answer every question, but to intrigue an employer. It cannot and should not attempt to substitute for you or totally summarize you!

The Importance of Visual and Mechanical Elements

A successful résumé gets read. Unless your résumé is attractive and inviting to an employer, it may be quickly dismissed. The most average credentials presented in an impressive way will always receive more initial attention than outstanding credentials poorly presented. Every job hunter owes it to himself to take pains with the visual and mechanical aspects of his résumé; the results will capture the employer's attention and predispose him favorably. The substantive text of your résumé may present problems for an employer, but the visual elements never should.

Margins

For maximum reader eye ease, a résumé must be centered on the page. Whatever your format, allow enough room for proper margins. Use the following approximate guidelines: 1½ inches at the top and bottom, 1–1½ inches on the left, 1–1½ on the right. And keep your margin line consistent, especially on the right side.

By centering your text and having adequate margins you will avoid some of the most common errors. Examples of these follow.

THE CROWDED RÉSUMÉ

Responsibilities Analyzed and wrote job descriptions and established standards for all departments. Evaluated jobs according to both a point factor comparison method and the Hay System. Adviser for Wage and Salary Administration, Employment, and Training. Conducted organizational and skill studies for job restructuring and the creation of career ladders and lattices. Performed the major training function for the department. Recommended changes in compensation based upon job requirements.
Key Accomplishments
*Reevaluated jobs to ensure internal equity among jobs and competitiveness with outside pay levels.
*Designed the job analysis training sessions for more than 100 employees which resulted in the decentralization of the job analysis function.
*Applied an in-depth knowledge of the Dictionary of Occupational Titles by preparing the Bankwide Job Analysis Handbook, Career

Scaffolding Information System, and other materials and studies related to occupational development.
*Counseled individuals on career opportunities and developed career reference materials.
*Conducted a needs analysis program with more than 20 group personnel officers which influenced '76 management objectives.
*Developed an evaluation system to correspond to the "task analysis" method of writing jobs.
*Promoted to employee relations representative after a relatively short period of time because of outstanding performance.

THE LOPSIDED RÉSUMÉ Too much space is wasted on the left side while the right side is crowded. Note how your eye focuses first on the dates rather than the text.

1985–1987   New York University, New York
                                   City, N.Y. University College of
                                   Arts and Science B.A. in Sociology
                                   and Urban Planning Assistant Edi-
                                   tor of student magazine Grade
                                   Point Average: 3.7 on 4 point scale
                                   Graduated*magna cum laude* and
                                   received Founders Day Honors
                                   Award

THE UNEVEN MARGIN A ragged right-hand margin will dramatically reduce the résumé's visual appeal. Make certain there is a *good* one-inch border on the right side.

For past 25 years active in several
community groups related to education,
child welfare, child protection,
social welfare, human relations, etc.
Extensive experience as public speaker
in field of social welfare to community and statewide groups including
speaker at sessions of the American
Public Welfare Association northeast
region.

Paper and Typeface

Use only bond paper with a cotton rag content. Do *not* use Corrasable, onionskin, or any other inexpensive typing paper. Bond paper is easy to obtain from any stationery store, offset printer, or college bookstore.

The proper paper weight for a résumé is sixteen or twenty pounds. Anything heavier, while elegant, is unnecessary and even pretentious.

The correct size paper is 8½ × 11 inches. Type on one side of the page only. Do *not* use legal-size paper or paper that will have to be folded.

Use either white paper or the very pale eggshell associated with wedding invitations. Do not try to distinguish yourself by using light green, yellow, gray, or dark beige paper.

Your résumé originally should be set to type or produced by a topnotch word processor or typewriter. Do not use a portable electric typewriter or a standard machine—they will not produce a sufficiently attractive page. A black typewriter ribbon is most correct, although brown can be attractive with ecru-colored paper. When in doubt, be conservative.

These seemingly minor details are so important that they can determine whether you look like a professional or an amateur.

Length

The ideal résumé is a nicely full one page, but if it appears that you'll have to cut short your accomplishments, by all means go to two pages. Just make certain that you can justify each entry as important. If your résumé turns out to be only one and a quarter pages long, edit it to one page if possible.

Whatever you do, don't exceed two pages. Few employers have the patience or motivation to wade through this much information. A three- or four-page résumé suggests disorganization and a lack of priorities. (When job hunters are without direction, they often fall victim to the smorgasbord approach—"If I tell you everything about me maybe something will interest you.")

Layout

If your résumé is to be inviting and easily read, it must have a unified and pleasing layout. Six out of ten new professionals make serious mistakes in this area.

Layout involves the following matters: format (outline or narrative), headings, consistency of format, visual clarity, and simplicity. Let's examine a portion of a résumé written in narrative form:

> I was born in Portland, Maine, in 1965, the only child of Bill and Bertha. My father was a farmer. After graduating from Portland High School as class valedictorian, I went on to the University of Maine, where I majored in art history and graduated in June 1987 with a B.A. I received my degree *cum laude* and won departmental honors for the best senior essay.

Now here is the same material cast into outline form. Note how much easier it is to absorb the salient points:

EDUCATIONAL BACKGROUND

> University of Maine, Augusta, Maine
> B.A. *cum laude,* June 1987
> Major: Art History
> Honors: departmental honors
>   outstanding senior essay

The outline format is preferable because it reduces the narrative thought to its most succinct form. The reader does not have the time or interest to wade through the wordiness of a narrative presentation. Use the latter only where it seems logical, as in job descriptions; but even there organize the material into a highly succinct series of clauses or brief sentences (see p. 144).

Do not overdo the outline format by using numbers and letters that will make your résumé look like an outline. With prominent headings and a well-laid-out basic text, the résumé will be sufficiently easy to read without obtrusive guideposts.

In the following example, notice the visual awkwardness created by over-outlining:

Position: Editor

Duties and Responsibilities:

1. Researching and writing articles on these current personnel subjects:
   (a) EEO and Affirmative Action (Equal Employment Opportunity Act and Executive Orders involving Federal contractors).
   (b) Testing (legality of FSEE, etc.)
   (c) Teachers' and other public employees' rights (tenure, maternity rights, retirement).
   (d) Selection and Recruitment.
2. Researching and updating state public employee bargaining laws (including the N.J. Employer-Employee Relations Act).

Headings are a useful organizing tool. They are also an important visual cue for your reader, who should be able to locate any particular fact, such as your degree and university, instantly.

Ideally, your heading should be at the left margin rather

than in the center of the page where it is visually hard to locate. This is called an overhang margin.

Sufficient white space around a heading is essential. It should be separated from the entries before and after it by a doublespace.

In the following example, notice how the use of an overhang margin as well as sufficient blank space contribute to the pleasing visual effect:

UNDERGRADUATE EDUCATION

    Tulane University, New Orleans, Louisiana
    B.A. June 1988
    Major: Art History
    Minor: Psychology

MUSEUM ADMINISTRATION EXPERIENCE

    etc.

Here is a crowded heading, jammed into the text:

UNDERGRADUATE EDUCATION

    Tulane University, New Orleans, Louisiana
    B.A. June 1988
    Major: Art History
    Minor: Psychology
    MUSEUM ADMINISTRATION EXPERIENCE
    etc.

Another way to give headings prominence is to use capital letters and to underline them. Notice the contrast between:

PROFESSIONAL SOCIAL WORK EDUCATION

and

    Professional Social Work Education

If you use caps and underlining for your headings, you will not use them elsewhere in your text, lest the reader's eye be pulled in too many directions. Keep your visual cues easy to see by highlighting only the headings. (Of course, some items on your résumé, such as *magna cum laude,* should be underlined, but keep the underlining to a minimum.)

The kind of layout you adopt for the top of your résumé should also be used at the bottom, even if the detail differs widely. A unified layout will make your text pleasing to the eye.

If one heading is in capital letters and underlined, all the rest should be. If you use an overhang margin at the top, use it at the bottom. Use your eye as the best judge of a unified page. For a good example, see pp. 119–20.

If the thought you are expressing exceeds one line of the résumé, indent the second line slightly so that the reader will not think the line begins a new entry. This minor detail can seriously affect the readability of your résumé. Notice how confusing the following entry is:

UNDERGRADUATE EDUCATION

    Massachusetts Institute of Technology, Cambridge, Massachusetts.
    Bachelor of Arts in Electrical Engineering, June 1988 *magna cum laude*
    Honors: Dwight Frank Scholar, 1987–88; departmental award for best honors thesis of a graduating senior

In the revised version, not only have the continuation lines been indented but perfectly clear abbreviations have reduced the need for many of them. Use a second line only where necessary.

UNDERGRADUATE EDUCATION

    Massachusetts Institute of Technology, Cambridge, Mass.

B.A. *magna cum laude,* June 1988
Major: Electrical Engineering
Honors: Dwight Frank Scholar, 1987–88; departmental
    award for outstanding honors thesis

Avoid needless clutter. For example, "Résumé of John Smith" is unnecessary—obviously, the reader has a résumé in his hands. Simply put your name at the top center of the page so someone will have a fighting chance of finding and remembering it.

Stay with a simple format. This horizontal effect is disconcerting:

Herbert H. Lehman College	Non-Matriculated Student School of General Studies	Certified License
City University of New York, Bedford Parkway	Teaching Courses for State & City Certified License	Candidate
Bronx, N.Y. 10468	(evening classes)	
9/84–5/86		

Avoid "framing" your text by putting the separate sections into boxes, as in the following example:

FRAME

> EDUCATION:

Although this effect was chosen to improve visual clarity, it is obtrusive and superfluous. A unified layout with prominent headings will make your résumé sufficiently clear.

Private résumé services seem to favor elaborate formats and hyperbole which invariably backfire with employers who rightly assume that intelligent professionals should be capable of writing their own straightforward, factual résumés. Fancy effects, dramatic headings such as "Others Have Said" (followed by a page of positively glowing but unattributed quotes) are visual and textual conceits that are dead giveaways of a ghost-written résumé. You can pay a great deal of money for bad advice that will end up making you look naïve to employers.

Ways to Reproduce Your Résumé

No employer expects to receive an "original" rather than a copy of your résumé. More important, no one is impressed by it.

There are several ways to reproduce your résumé effectively. Whatever method you choose, *proofread carefully.* There is nothing more annoying than discovering a typographical error duplicated onto a hundred résumés and being forced to choose between spending another ten dollars to redo them or ruining the professional effect you have taken pains to create.

Do not make more copies than you need right now. Since most résumés need updating every three or four months, you'll undoubtedly want new copies made then. Typed addenda are almost as bad as typos. Plan to redo your résumé frequently.

For more than thirty-five copies, photo offset is probably the best technique. Shop around for quality and price. A list of printers is readily found in the yellow pages of your telephone directory.

Typically a printer who regularly services résumé writers will have a good selection of bond papers available. If not, buy your paper and bring it.

The cheapest method for reproducing small quantities of résumés, thirty-five or fewer, is probably to photocopy. Choose a place that has a reputation for fine work. Usually a business area is a better bet than a university neighborhood.

Because the machine may be having a bad day, check the quality of one copy before you place a sizable order and get stuck with a hundred copies that have black dots. A résumé should be visually perfect.

How to Write an Effective Résumé

Now let us proceed step by step through the actual writing of your résumé. Plan to set aside a few hours of uninterrupted time when you feel fresh and motivated. Employers will prefer the résumé that will emerge to the more typical generalized and chronological résumé your classmates will probably use.

A relevant or focused résumé addresses the specific needs and interests of its intended audience by organizing and patterning detail into relevant categories. It puts chronological events into a meaningful structure, whereas a general résumé clumps all education into "Education" and all experience, relevant or not, into "Employment."

Here are some other important characteristics of the relevant résumé:

1. You highlight details relevant to your employment goals and minimize those that are not. Thus a part-time job from five years ago might be given more space than a current job.

2. You suggest future effectiveness by stressing past effectiveness.

3. You make your experience constitute a bridge to the future rather than a mere summary of your past, espe-

cially if the past is now irrelevant, as in the case of a career changer.

4. You reach out to the employer by using the vocabulary of the working world whenever possible and making your experience specific—by saying "Real Estate Employment" rather than "Employment," for example.

5. You shape lifeless facts into cogent themes and patterns that will be of interest to your readers.

6. You make apparently unrelated experience newly pertinent by stressing transferable skills.

This kind of résumé can be an important learning exercise for you. If you are inexperienced in your field, it will help you to clarify marketable strengths and decide which employers you wish to attract. If you are changing careers, it may be an important first step in asserting your new professional identity to yourself and the world; it may also help you to be perceived in terms of your future, rather than your former career. If you are unemployed or underemployed, it will help to focus attention on your professional credentials rather than your current status.

The General versus the Relevant Résumé

Ann Ambitious is a young woman in search of a job as a budget analyst in the public sector. She has no full-time experience in her field but does have a master's in public administration. In comparing her two résumés, imagine yourself as her prospective employer.

General Résumé

ANN AMBITIOUS

CURRENT ADDRESS
105 West 79th Street
New York, N.Y. 10019
212-686-0985

PERSONAL DATA
Date of Birth: 5/2/65
Marital Status: Single
Health: Excellent

PROFESSIONAL EDUCATION

New York University Graduate School of Public Administration, N.Y.
M.P.A. June 1988
Program: Urban Public Policy
Honors and Awards: Lesley Jane Rosen Scholar, 1986–88

UNDERGRADUATE EDUCATION

Ohio State University, Columbus, Ohio
B.A. *magna cum laude,* June 1986
Major: Political Science
Minor: Economics
Honors: Phi Beta Kappa

EMPLOYMENT

Office of Management and Budget, New York City
Position: NYU Intern Spring 1988

Bill's Sweet Shoppe, Columbus, Ohio
Position: Waitress Summers 1985, 1986

Ohio State University, Columbus, Ohio
Position: Researcher, Political Science Dept. 1984–86 (part-time)

Ohio State *Lantern,* Columbus, Ohio
Position: Business Manager 1983–85

Ohio State University Libraries
Position: Library Clerk 1982–83

Camp Chawinga, Albany, N.Y.
Position: Camp Counselor Summers 1980, 1981, 1982

REFERENCES

References will be furnished upon request.

Relevant Résumé

ANN AMBITIOUS

CURRENT ADDRESS	PERSONAL DATA
105 West 79th Street	Date of Birth: 5/2/65
New York, New York 10019	Marital Status: Single
212-686-0985	Health: Excellent
	Languages: Fluent Spanish

PUBLIC ADMINISTRATION EDUCATION

New York University Graduate School of Public Administration, N.Y.
M.P.A. June 1988
Course Concentration: Budgeting and Finance

Special Skills: Statistics and Computers
Cumulative Average: 3.7/4.0
Honors and Awards: Lesley Jane Rosen Scholar, 1986–88
Internship: New York City Office of Management and Budget, 1977

UNDERGRADUATE EDUCATION

Ohio State University, Columbus, Ohio
B.A. *magna cum laude,* June 1986
Major: Political Science
Minor: Economics
Honors: Phi Beta Kappa
        Political Science Honorary Society
        Who's Who Among American College Freshmen
Activities: President, Political Science Honorary Society Academic
        Affairs Committee, Department of Political Science
Research Assistant: Department of Political Science, 1984–86

BUDGETING EXPERIENCE

Office of Management and Budget, New York City
Position: NYU Intern Spring 1988
Duties: Worked as team member on budget evaluation of major NYC
agency; prepared statistical data and first draft for final report; supervised three other student interns.

Ohio State *Lantern* (daily newspaper)
Position: Business Manager (September 1983–June 1985)
Duties: Supervised all business and budgeting responsibilities for
school daily with a circulation of 35,000. Increased revenues by 20%
by increasing advertising space; reduced operating costs by 30%;
total operating budget yearly: $75,000.

OTHER EMPLOYMENT

Earned approximately 40% of undergraduate and graduate school
expenses through a variety of part-time and summer employment
including: waitress, research assistant, camp counselor, and library
attendant.

REFERENCES

References will be furnished upon request.

In her relevant résumé, note the following details:

Amplified Graduate Study

Ann made her graduate study look unusually important by amplifying it. Adding categories such as "course concentration" and "specific skills" makes her look like an interesting and interested bright beginner. It also catches the attention of her audience.

Clear Budgeting Theme

Notice how the budgeting theme appears throughout the résumé, first as a course concentration, then as an internship, and lastly as a heading to organize two relevant previous jobs. The use of a theme highlights her identity as a "budget person" to her audience.

Format for Graduate Educational Data

Ann described her graduate education separately from her undergraduate education; she used "Public Administration Education" because she wished to draw attention to those specific credentials that would help her. Had her undergraduate training been more pertinent (e.g., accounting), she would have put them together.

Undergraduate Education

Notice how the order of entries in the undergraduate education sections follows the preceding graduate entry. The school is listed first, then the degree, date, and major field of study. This helps to unify the résumé both visually and textually.

The elaborate account of activities at Ohio State is presented largely because Ann lacked professional experience. An important principle of the relevant résumé is to make the most of whatever positive data you have. Two years from now Ann would stress work experience rather than undergraduate activities. But for now, it reinforces the image of vitality she is trying to project.

Specific Functional Headings

The functional heading "Budgeting Experience" is an important cue to an employer, who is bound to respond with interest to the focus on his needs. It is significant, however, that her entire budgeting experience consists of an internship and a college part-time job! By amplifying and highlighting her slight credentials, Ann is not misrepresenting herself. She is approaching her résumé creatively by making the most of the skills and background she has to offer. This helps to underscore her professional commitment.

Skill-Oriented Job Descriptions

Moreover, with skill-oriented job descriptions that emphasized her accomplishments, she was able to demonstrate a results-oriented attitude that suggests an effective worker.

Assigning Priorities to Experience

Equally impressive was her selective way of dealing with jobs that didn't involve budgeting. "Other Employment" is a useful general heading that can include a full-time job. Note, too, her rationale for these jobs: she quite rightly called attention to her motivation rather than to the details of irrelevant and fairly menial jobs.

How to Create Your Own Relevant Résumé

To make your résumé relevant, first identify the specific job you want. For example, a social worker might choose a psychiatric social work position in a voluntary hospital in Chicago. A forthcoming lawyer might want to be an environmental lawyer in a public interest firm in the Northwest. And a teacher might choose to teach Russian and French at community colleges or private high schools anywhere. In each instance, there is some obvious specialization within a general professional field.

The next step is to *list your credentials.* This sheet will constitute the data you will be working with as you actually draft your résumé according to the directions listed in the next section.

Academic Training: List your academic qualifications briefly such as graduate and/or undergraduate training, related degrees, certificate programs, licenses, workshops, clinics, short courses, or independent study.

Practical Experience: Jot down any related practical experience, whether or not it was for pay. Consider volunteer experience, research experience, and extracurricular activities in graduate or undergraduate school as likely sources of related experience. Do not overlook academic reports, special academic workshops, or practicums. Related tasks in a civic or religious capacity count too.

Before you move into the next category, review all of the summer and part-time jobs you have had along the way for evidence of pertinent professional skills, even if only tangentially related. For example, Ann Ambitious might have helped on the budget as a senior camp counselor; being a counselor is hardly pertinent, but the budgeting skills are transferable.

Skills: Professional skills can range from general, such as writing, analytical, research, and oral communication skills, to the specific skills identified with your profession, such as accounting, textual analysis, or quantitative methods. If you are in doubt about which skills your audience will consider relevant, find the answers now.

You may have multiple goals that are not particularly compatible—to be a budget analyst with a public agency and a university fundraiser, for example. If so, write two relevant résumés, since the fundraisers won't appreciate receiving a budget-analyst résumé, or vice versa.

If you are clear about your career direction, there is no need to write a general résumé in addition to a relevant one. However, for people with fairly broad degrees or complex backgrounds, a general résumé might also be helpful. Write such a résumé after you have written the more focused one. And only duplicate about ten copies.

Now that you have identified your audience and assembled the pertinent data, let's write your résumé, using Ann Ambitious as a visual guide.

The order we will follow will not necessarily reflect *your* final order. Use your own judgment in deciding whether to list experience before education or vice versa. Always list the most pertinent strengths first: relevant full-time job experience in your desired field, if you have it; otherwise, your graduate and/or undergraduate study.

The "required" résumé elements are:

1. name, address, and telephone
2. selected personal data
3. graduate education
4. undergraduate education (may be combined with # 3)
5. professional or related experience

6. other employment
7. references

The optional elements are:

8. publications and papers
9. professional memberships and affiliations
10. hobbies
11. job or career objective
12. summary

Name, Address, and Telephone

Your *name, address,* and a *telephone number* (where the phone will be answered during the business day) should be at the top of the first page. If you are at a temporary address and may soon be moving, include a permanent address as well. Be clear.

Whether or not you are relocating, a telephone number where you can be reached is critical information since many employers with immediate openings invariably telephone for an interview. And they may not call back twice on a busy morning.

One solution is to use an inexpensive answering service for three or four months. It is a wise investment for a serious job hunter who doesn't want to sit by the phone or buy a machine.

Another solution is to indicate your availability in one of the following possible ways:

(212) 833-2975 (after 6:00 P.M.)

(212) 833-2975
(212) 833-6045 (leave messages)

(212) 833-2975 (mornings only)

Personal Data

What constitutes *personal data* is a matter of interpretation. Think of this category as a vehicle for communicating pieces of useful information to an employer, such as your willingness to relocate or pertinent language skills, rather than the state of your health, other strictly personal information, or revealing details that could be used against you unfairly, such as a religious affiliation.

Generally, personal data should be put at the top right of your résumé (see Ann Ambitious) or as a separate section near the bottom of the résumé. Three to five entries are enough; type entries single space. Do not follow Bill Brown's example:

BILL BROWN

Address: 1401 Hollow Court, Arlington, Va.
Telephone: (304) 262-6784
Date of Birth: May 29, 1963
Place of Birth: New York City
Height: 6'1" Weight: 175
Citizenship: United States
Marital Status: Married
Wife's Name: Ann Brown
Health: Excellent

In selecting appropriate personal data, review the following lists. Starred items are ones that employers cannot legally inquire about. Decide for yourself about including them. Employers are always interested in such information.

OPTIONAL DATA

- dates of degrees
- date of birth
- marital status

- children
- place of birth
- nationality or work permit
- special skills or languages
- relocation information (if pertinent: "desired location: Denver")
- health (only if excellent)
- hobbies or travel (if pertinent)
- availability ("immediately" or the date, "July 15," may be helpful)
- height and weight (unless you are entering a beauty contest)
- name and/or occupation of spouse
- religious beliefs
- political beliefs
- dates of birth or education
- military status

Select entries with two goals in mind: to emphasize strengths and to think defensively. And always avoid data that will trigger problems with an employer. For example, the single New York City woman wishing to relocate to rural Vermont will not be taken seriously ("Why would a single woman want to come here?"). She should add "will relocate" to the personal data and possibly go so far as to state: "Preferred location: Vermont." Other examples of thinking defensively are:

Are you separated or divorced? There may be a stigma to saying so candidly, so merely say "single." Or omit it, because your marital status is no one's business, according to law.

Are you a woman with small children? The employer may worry about how responsible you'll be and whether or not you'll be able to work overtime when necessary. Rather than listing the names and ages of your children, do not mention them or merely note, "two children." Then, during the interview, be prepared to say, "My husband and I have worked out good childcare arrangements. If you are concerned about overtime, you need not be."

Are you a divorced woman with small children? This is an emotion-laden image for a male employer. Either say "single" or leave out marital/children data altogether.

Do you have health problems? At nineteen, Bill Smith, a graduate of Princeton and a law review editor, had some heart surgery. Under the personal-data section of his résumé, he listed the long Latin medical name for his heart ailment.

Despite his outstanding academic record, not one law firm out of forty he had canvassed requested a personal interview. When asked if his ailment would adversely affect his job performance, he decisively answered, "No." Yet in the interest of an almost self-destructive honesty, this misguided applicant had included an alarming medical term that spelled instant death for his résumé. The proper context for such information is an interview, where it can be explained.

If your health is excellent, say so explicitly.

Are you an alien or do you have a foreign name? Employers will immediately worry about your work permit or fluency in English. To assuage such fears, set up the personal-data section at the top right-hand corner of your résumé, to emphasize elements that will set their fears to rest:

HALIT ZAZOUR

PERSONAL DATA

Date of Birth: 5/29/62
Citizenship: U.S.
Languages: Fluent and accentless English; Arabic [or bilingual English/Arabic]
Place of Birth: Istanbul, Turkey

However, if you have degrees from U.S. schools, such defensive detail will not be necessary. Employers will assume you are fluent.

Hobbies: Hobbies can be an item under Personal Data. However, they are often too personal to warrant placement at the top corner of your résumé.

Hobbies are generally more effective with small-town employers, who are usually more interested in applicants as people than are big-city employers. On the other hand, any employer will find your Boston Marathon participation or your pilot's license intriguing.

Avoid ubiquitous general hobbies such as "theater, travel, and reading." If intellectual interests will be an asset, mention Greek drama or Victorian novels specifically. Not music, but Wagner. Try to strike a balance between being interesting and being a good "fit" with others in your field.

Again, it's wise to think defensively. Small-town lawyers don't take kindly to a thirty-one-year-old bachelor who lists bread baking, modern dance, and Zen.

Hobbies can also serve as interview fodder. For example, sailing might intrigue Rhode Islanders, an interest in antiques might interest New Englanders, and Californians are likely to identify with surfing.

Religious affiliations: Religion is irrelevant unless you are applying to a religious organization. If your religious beliefs will restrict your ability to work normal business hours, save such information for the interview.

Political affiliations: Sometimes people obtain important and transferable professional skills from political work. These are worth emphasizing. Otherwise your political activities may not be relevant or helpful with employers of opposing views unless you worked for a prominent senator or were in office yourself.

Dates of birth or education: Don't add dates unless you want someone to calculate your age. If you face the prospect of age discrimination, you might do well to eliminate clues since a degree date is a dead giveaway.

Military status: Vietnam veterans are often viewed with suspicion (unlike earlier groups of veterans) due to the percentage of drug abusers in this group.

Graduate Education

Arrange résumé material about your *graduate education* in reverse chronological order. Put your most recent graduate degree first, before your undergraduate degree. Highlight the most relevant credential immediately, lest the employer be unable to find this important fact easily or lose interest in you.

First select a heading that will help to establish immediate common ground with the employer. Opt for the specific vocabulary that will describe you as a professional rather than as a student. For example, pick "Legal Education," "Professional Social Work Training," or "Graduate Business Education" rather than the vaguer "Educational Background" or "Professional Education." Here you introduce the theme of John Brown—motivated, effective, and skilled professional.

The exact wording of *your* heading may vary considerably. Apart from selecting the proper terminology for your own field, consider the rhythm and visual pattern formed by the words. For example, with Ann Ambitious, "Public Administration Education" was selected as a more graceful alternative to the otherwise acceptable "Professional Public Administration Education." Use the adjectives "graduate" or "professional" if possible. "Graduate Legal Education" implies a master's in law rather than a J.D., however.

The next step is to list and describe the details of your graduate education. First, list the full name and location of your school but omit lengthy addresses and abbreviate where possible. In the following example, the first is good, the second even better because it eliminates the second line.

New York University Graduate School of Public
Administration, N.Y., N.Y.

N.Y.U. Graduate School of Public Administration, N.Y., N.Y.

There is no need to give a complete street address or zip code:

New York University Graduate School of Public Administration
4 Washington Square North
N.Y., N.Y. 10003

However, always state the division as well as the university. Just "New York University" is not enough.

The next entry is your degree, its date or expected date (assuming you wish to put dates), and any graduation honors.

Tulane University, New Orleans, La.
B.A. *magna cum laude,* June 1988

Always write out a degree that might not be fully understood, such as a new or very specialized degree. For example: M.H.S. (Master of Human Services), M.L.A. (Master of Liberal Arts).

If you have further specialization within your course of study, mention that program. For example, a person with an

M.P.A. may have been enrolled in either an international relations or health planning program.

Consider whether or not the school's terminology for a particular course of study or program transfers well to employers. You will not misrepresent if you adopt or change the words to suit your audience, such as "Real Estate Law" instead of its academic equivalent, "Land Use Regulation." Always use the practical word rather than the academic wherever possible.

In the following examples, the first is vague, the second revelant:

> *Health Policy Planning and Administration* vs. *Hospital Administration* or *Health Planning* (*Note:* the latter are also job titles)
> *Urban Public Policy* vs. *Financial Management* (*Note:* the latter is more specific and is also a practical job title)
> *Social Work Theory and Practice* vs. *Psychiatric Social Work*
> *Philosophy of Law* vs. *Jurisprudence*

Now let's turn to a group of optional entries that can give your education market appeal. Select only those items that will give you a chance to emphasize your unique strengths, and omit the others. You may, for example, want to omit your cumulative average but emphasize special skills.

Aim for comprehensiveness at the outset. Don't worry about excessive detail. After you have typed a preliminary résumé draft, you can weed out items of lesser importance.

SPECIAL SKILLS. Select one to three. Include such "soft" but pertinent skills as research, writing, or public relations, or "hard" skills such as accounting, or demographic analysis. Select skills you know to be pertinent to *your* desired job or to the needs of employers in *your* field. Good writing skills, for example, may be less pertinent than your statistical skills.

How much training constitutes a skill? One course at the graduate level or two courses at the undergraduate constitutes a reasonable minimum. If you have taught yourself basic accounting and used it effectively in graduate studies, this is a perfectly legitimate skill to include. Once again, your own judgment is the best guide. Avoid omitting skills because you are modest. Any employer who wants to test your skill can do so through a few probing interview questions. Avoid the embarrassment of a fellow who listed his knowledge of German but failed to note it was solely a reading knowledge. He was subsequently interviewed in German for an international relations job!

COURSE CONCENTRATION. Begin by reviewing your specific job-hunting goals as you choose one to three possible entries for your course concentration. For example, a person with a master's in engineering may be seeking a job specifically in noise control or transportation. These would become his course concentration. Start with your goals and then backtrack to your credentials.

Even if you have not previously thought about your studies in such specific terms, do so now. At this early point, Ann Ambitious signaled her goal of budget professional. She added finance as a second concentration, thinking it would help her. If you have already used the word "program" to give clarity to a generalized degree, you may still refer to "course concentration." The two are not mutually exclusive. In choosing your entries, always consider their impact upon your intended audience.

The definition of a proper course concentration is fairly subjective. If your graduate program is one year in length, as few as two courses might legitimately suffice; those in a two- or three-year program should have had three to five courses. Once again, make a reasonable judgment, and do not worry about misrepresentation. If you feel that your course concentration cannot be quite as specific as your job-hunting goals, be more general. You will at least point your reader in the general direction of your concerns.

In choosing your entries, keep the employer's concerns uppermost in mind. For example, "family therapy" is more specific and has greater market appeal than "group counseling." Always consider what will make an employer interview you, whether citing a general area such as "public interest law" or a specific expertise, such as "environmental law." If you list three items, strive for a balance between specific expertise and general training.

Finally, if the term "course concentration" is not the most appropriate for you, feel free to alter it. A college teacher with a Ph.D. in history could use the traditional terms "major fields" and "minor fields" instead.

SPECIAL AREA(S) OF INTEREST. Areas of interest are a good alternative to citing a course concentration, since one can be interested in criminal justice planning without having the expertise associated with an academic concentration.

If you have indicated a course concentration in museum administration, you may now wish to point to specific special interests within that area.

Here's an example of how a detailed account of your graduate training alone can establish you as an interesting professional to an employer:

New York University Graduate School of Public
Administration
M.P.A. June 1988

Course Concentration: Museum Administration
Special Skills: Budgeting and Fundraising
Special Areas of Interest: Crafts and Folk Art

You may use the term "Other Areas of Interest" when you wish to emphasize range and diversity. For example:

M.B.A. June 1988
Course Concentration: Investment Banking
Special Skills: Economic Analysis
Other Areas of Interest: Management

CLASS RANK AND/OR CUMULATIVE AVERAGE. Typically, these must be impressive to warrant listing—at least a B+ average (3.3 on a 4.0 scale) or "upper third" of class rank. But if it is common practice in your field to list grades, then do so unless you want employers to assume that yours are unmentionably poor.

In listing your grade-point average, always compare it to a perfect grade average thus: 3.3/4.0. Or write: "3.4 (4.0=A)." You can also use letters. If you don't know how to compute your grade-point average accurately, ask the registrar at your graduate school. Or indicate "approximately 3.3/4.0" or "approximately B+."

GRADUATE RECORD SCORES. Scores of any sort are usually left out of résumés, unless you are a first-year graduate student looking for summer employment or have extremely high scores but little actual experience. If you do have experience, why include scores used to predict success?

HONORS AND AWARDS. List honors and awards received as a graduate student in the detail about graduate school and not as a separate section. Prospective employers cannot be expected to grasp the full significance of some awards you may have received. For example, there is no way that an employer will know the Henry Wiggins Award was for the highest grade-point average in your graduating class. As you jot down entries for this section, clarity and economy of presentation should be your two goals. For example:

Honors and Awards: Martin Smith Award for Outstanding
                     Leadership
                     HEW Title IX Award (full scholarship)

Be succinct; weigh the need for annotation against the unattractiveness of clutter. Instead of the wordy and unnecessary

Honors and Awards: Presidential Management Intern
                     Nominee
                     (One of the eighteen people
                     nominated by the school)

consider the succinct alternative:

Honors and Awards: Presidential Management Intern
                     Nominee.

ACTIVITIES. Few graduate students have many activities. But if you have, do list them. Election as a university senator or member of a faculty-student council is sufficiently impressive. Even "Business School basketball team" can be a graceful detail that helps to suggest a well-rounded personality, not all work and no play. Omit such nebulous activities as the spring bake sale, or the classic aggrandizement, "Chairman, Poster Committee for Spring Dance."

If you are a minority student and member of an organized minority group, your decision to include such detail should be based upon a larger philosophical decision of whether or not to emphasize your racial background.

Women active in a school feminist organization should

similarly evaluate their chosen audience. Employers in large cities might not blink at feminist affiliations, but stereotypical reactions to "women's libbers" could emerge in conservative or rural areas.

INTERNSHIPS, RESEARCH EXPERIENCE, PRACTICUMS, WORKSHOPS, OR CLINICS. Practical experience should be first mentioned succinctly here and then possibly expanded upon again as "experience" later.

Here are a few examples of the succinct style in which such material should be listed:

Research Assistant: Professor Harriet Stengels' study of violent adolescents, spring 1986

Relevant Practicum: Family Therapy practicum, spring 1987

SELECTED PAPERS OR PUBLICATIONS. If as a graduate student you have written some intriguing papers or developed some noteworthy expertise, including these data will suggest strong writing skills. More than two or three entries, however, would warrant a separate section and heading.

OTHER POSSIBLE ENTRIES. If the preceding discussion has excluded a category you think will help you, by all means add it now. Your résumé should be a flexible tool that can readily be adapted to the demands of your job campaign or personal history.

PREVIOUS ADVANCED DEGREE. A previous advanced degree should be kept firmly in the background; your Ph.D. in philosophy may threaten the impact of your new M.B.A. Sometimes, however, the two degrees in combination constitute a market advantage, such as a Ph.D./M.A.; M.B.A./ J.D.; M.P.A./M.B.A. But if you obtained the new graduate degree in the hope of changing career direction, then deemphasize the old advanced degree by putting it at the end of your résumé. One way is to list your graduate education first, next your relevant experience, and then create a category called "Other Education" for your old advanced degree and your undergraduate one.

To ascertain how employers will view your old degree, ask your placement director and working professionals in your new field. They will talk frankly about the prejudice of hospital administrators against hiring those with a therapy or nursing background or the skepticism of businessmen toward a Ph.D. Your acceptance of these realities and the decision to plan defensively may mean the difference between success and failure.

Your Undergraduate Education

You must decide first whether to list your undergraduate degree under the same heading that you used for graduate education. The alternative is to create a new section, "Undergraduate Education." If, for example, you have a M.S.W. and your undergraduate major was also social work, put both under the same heading. Prevent crowding by allowing two lines between the entries. If an undergraduate economics major is an extra asset for an M.B.A., put the two together. When in doubt, however, always list the undergraduate degree separately.

You can now move on to listing the necessary specifics. Just as you did with your graduate education, write the name of your university and then your degree and year. At this point, however, add the listing "Major" followed by "Minor," if pertinent. You will not use "program" or "course concentration."

Next review possible optional entries. The items listed are the same ones used with your graduate education. Exclude the bulleted items unless you find them extremely pertinent.

- Special Skills
  Cumulative Grade Average (and/or class rank)
- Special Areas of Interest
  Honors and Awards
  Activities
  Internships
- Selected papers
- Other entries

Specific guidelines are discussed on pp. 133–38. Since activities are often an important factor in undergraduate experience, highlight them by listing the most impressive ones first. Always emphasize any leadership role:

> *Activities:* President, Senate Judiciary Board
> Secretary, Student Association

There is no need to indicate transfer or nondegree study unless it is pertinent. If you do, make the entry brief and succinct. For example:

UNDERGRADUATE EDUCATION

> University of Michigan, Ann Arbor, Michigan
> B.A. June 1988
>
> Duke University, Chapel Hill, N.C.
> Attended: 1984–86
> Major: Economics

Cumulative average, honors, awards, and activities should only be listed if they are very impressive.

Do not include data about high school unless you attended a famous high school or are applying for a job near where you attended high school, such as a Californian who attended Phillips Exeter Academy and then returned to California for all other schooling. At graduation time, when he decided to apply in the New England region, Exeter helped to establish the credibility of his New England job search.

Professional or Related Experience

To an employer, experience is the most pivotal and interesting section of your résumé. This is where your creativity in selecting pertinent facts from your background will be critical.

What constitutes experience? Here are some of the possibilities:

Full-time paid experience
Part-time paid experience
Internship
Research experience for a professor or organization
Volunteer work
Civic activities of substance
Any workshops, practicums, or similar academic
 coursework with practical tasks

The first step is to establish common ground with employers by creating headings that link up with career goals. Such typical headings as "Employment Background" or "Experience" fail to suggest any sense of professional direction or priorities. Everything under "Employment" must be lumped together in reverse chronological order, as if it were all of equivalent importance. Consider that the employer must wade through such material and hunt for what is pertinent.

Show your ability to organize by creating relevant headings, as Ann Ambitious did with her "Budget Experience."
She organized her limited previous experience as an intern
and newspaper business editor in a meaningful way. She also
reduced emphasis on chronology.

Your first heading should repeat general or specific words
connected with your job search. For example, a law student
will choose the general-sounding "Legal Experience" or
"Law-related Experience" or the more specific "Litigation
Experience" or "Corporate Commercial Law." Depending
upon his goals, the teacher with a master's in education
seeking an elementary school teaching job might pick a heading "Elementary Teaching Experience" or the more general
"Teaching Experience." A person seeking a job in business
might choose the general heading "Business Experience" or
specific headings such as "Business Employment," "Marketing Employment," or "Retailing Background." The more
relevant your headings are to one audience, the less relevant
they will be to another. Be sure to take this into consideration.

You may quite rightly respond, "But I have no experience!
I can't dream up fantastical headings!" Are you certain you
are looking hard enough for at least related experience? An
experience qualifies as "related" if it is tangentally related or
if you have practiced relevant skills (e.g., the newspaper
business manager who handled a budget).

If, after careful examination, you find no experience to
describe in a relevant heading, you have two other options.
Either select headings that emphasize relevant skills for your
field, such as "Research Experience" or "Writing Background," or find a term that is both fair and relevant. For
example, for a woman who has been primarily a wife and
mother, the term "Family Administration Background" is

an effective heading. It forces an employer to sit up and take notice of her organizational skills, instead of instantly stereotyping her. If she had substantive civic involvement, she could use "Civic Affairs Background." Make your past work for your future. Do not disregard its potential value.

Organize all your experience in one to three sections, with the most relevant first, as did this social worker:

> Social Work Experience
> Other Employment

If you have had experience in an area that will be an asset to your primary goal, emphasize it, as did this university administrator:

> University Administrative Experience
> College Teaching Experience
> Other Employment

If you prefer, you can combine two kinds of experience:

> Research and Policy Analysis Experience

For brevity, omit "and" and insert a slash mark:

> Research/Policy Analysis Experience

Write *effective job descriptions.* Start with the employer's name, city, and address. To include street address and zip code would be unnecessarily detailed:

> Brookdale Senior Citizens Center, Detroit, Michigan

Next list your title and position. If necessary, alter the title to do justice to reality. For example, a secretary who runs a large office might well describe herself as an "office manager" rather than as a secretary. She is *not* misrepresenting her actual job in altering her title. Make a vague job title specific so that employers will know what you do:

University of Illinois, Urbana, Illinois
Position: Director of Student Affairs (Housing and Student
   Activities)

List "Duties" or, still better, "Selected Accomplishments," and then choose among possible visual formats. These will emphasize your ability to achieve results and demonstrate transferable skills, rather than merely complete duties. However, sometimes it may seem more appropriate to call your work experience "duties" yet write them to stress skills and accomplishments.

Let's look at some:

In format #1 the job hunter had a part-time job in college that was pertinent to her desired career in management. She wrote it up in outline format and listed the most impressive results first.

FORMAT #1

Office of Management and Budget, N.Y.C.
Position: Assistant Analyst
Selected Accomplishments:
   • Worked as team member on pilot financial analysis of Queens.
      • Drafted section of final report on economic development.
      • Interviewed varied city officials.
      • Performed regression analysis.

The "bullets" were helpful visual devices that separated the highly compact text. If you use them for one job, use them for all. Such dots are created by a large "O" filled in with black ink. Always use large dots.

Format #2 is particularly useful for jobs with diversified duties. The use of capitals is justified here to draw attention to the skills.

FORMAT #2

Cullen, Bryant and Whitman Attorneys at Law, Boston, Mass.
Position: Law Clerk
Duties: LITIGATION: drafted interrogatories and motion papers; TAX: researched "section #362"; CORPORATE: drafted corporate minutes, formed a corporation, and assisted in registration statements.

As an example of the flexibility available to you in selecting a format for your job descriptions, refer back to how Ann Ambitious described her budget jobs. This is format #3, the one most frequently used.

There is a certain format you should avoid, although it is often suggested by counselors and organizations who deal with women going back to work. That is the résumé that lists a summary page or so of "skills" completely detached from any specific job context. Not only will an employer refuse to believe such a lengthy recital of skills but the lack of pertinent facts is apt to make him irate. You may be understandably dismissed as a disorganized person given to puffery.

A second format to avoid is the two-or-more-page résumé that begins with a one-page summary. A résumé should be a succinct document, not a tome that needs its own résumé!

It is important to indicate dates for any full or part-time experience that you are citing as relevant. But they should be unobtrusive and at the end of a job description, or to the right of the employer name. Too many people fill up their critical left margin with dates that are too prominent.

Be clear and succinct:

> Spring, 1988
> January, 1987–current
> 1/87–1/88

The length of job descriptions is an important issue. Do not be afraid that your job description will be too long. *Relevant* experience should be given the full treatment. Omit trivial details that merely pad out a description, such as "attended staff meetings." But do break up lengthy text into several short paragraphs of about six sentences. Indent for greater eye ease in reading. There is a special language for writing effective job descriptions. Here are a few tips.

1. Make descriptions of your duties and accomplishments specific. For example, state that you "directed an annual budget of 3 million dollars" rather than that you "were responsible for the budget." The bold "originated and administered a free-lunch program serving 21,000 schoolchildren" is a concrete result far better than the vague "developed a free-lunch program."

   Emphasize successes wherever pertinent. Say "wrote and obtained a $50,000 NIH grant" rather than "wrote grant proposals." If your research study was later cited by an official body as "distinguished," say so. If you developed a community program for 500 children, mention the number. Anchor your activities and accomplishments in the concrete and quantifiable.

2. Use strong active verbs to describe your duties and accomplishments. For example, stress your active in-

volvement by saying, "coordinated city-wide environmental programs" rather than the limp alternative, "responsible for the coordination of city-wide programs." Prepositional phrases cannot match the vigor of verbs.

3. Use parallel sentence structure. "*Organized* city-wide environmental efforts; *hired* staff for four poverty programs; *coordinated* all community outreach programs; *monitored* annual 4-million-dollar budget." If you write, "Organized city-wide effort; responsible for the hiring of all staff; implementing a budget of 4 million dollars" the variations in sentence structure make for a weak, hard-to-read description.

4. Use first person. Write your job descriptions in the first person: "*Direct* (or directed) a new department of community affairs." However, there is no need to add the pronoun "I." It is understood.

5. Avoid referring to yourself as "the writer": "The writer directed a new department of community affairs."

6. Clarify ambiguities. The effectiveness of your résumé hinges on its clarity. If your professional experience has been with an organization your audience won't know or whose function is not immediately clear, add a brief explanatory sentence or parenthetical note: "Abro Corporation, N.Y., N.Y. (computer software concern)."

7. Highlight past careers if transferable skills exist in past employment only peripherally related to your new career. In the following example, a would-be hospital administrator highlighted the administrative components in her former nursing career:

HOSPITAL ADMINISTRATIVE EXPERIENCE

Kings County Hospital, Brooklyn, N.Y.
Position: Head Nurse, Pediatrics
Duties and Accomplishments:

- Improved departmental efficiency by reorganizing personnel for greater productivity. Cut operating costs by 30% in one year.
- Developed new ombudsman project with ten volunteers. Later copied by five New York hospitals.
- Wrote and obtained HEW grant for $10,000 to develop peer counseling project in out-patient clinic.
- Devised monitoring system for ward.
- General nursing duties

8. Make volunteer experience relevant. Avoid the usual flat description of volunteer work:

CIVIC ACTIVITIES

Chairman, Brookdale Neighborhood Association
Member, Board of Directors
Parent Teacher Association, President

Here's an improved version of the first item:

RELEVANT ADMINISTRATIVE EXPERIENCE

Brookdale Neighborhood Association, Brookdale, Wis.
Position: Chairman
Duties: Organized the first block association network in state with fifty thousand members. Developed community outreach programs servicing a low-income population of one million. Established youth programs, volunteer urban corps, and senior citizens activities. Received HUD award for "leadership and innovation." Recipient of $200,000 in federal assistance funds.

References

At the end of your résumé state, "References will be furnished upon request."

If your references are "household words," include names. Be brief. One or two names are enough.

Publications or Relevant Papers, Reports, and Projects (Optional)

You need not actually have published to convey your writing interests and presumed skill. You can describe academic term papers as Special Reports. Alter or rearrange the heading as you see fit.

Professional Memberships (Optional)

If you have been a leader in any pertinent professional organization, list this membership and stress your role. But don't go overboard and list all organizations indiscriminately. A good rule of thumb is to decide whether listing the membership will help to compensate for lack of actual experience.

Hobbies

If you have a hobby that seems sufficiently important and pertinent to your career, by all means create a special section for it, "Relevant Hobbies."

Job or Career Objective

This term is defined as a one- or two-sentence description of a career or job goal. It generally appears at the very top of the résumé. It is useful to:

1. the career changer who wants to take no chance that anyone will confuse his or her present aspirations;

2. the person of greatly diversified background whose current direction may perplex some employers;

3. the out-of-state job hunter who wants to stress a desire to relocate to the specific state or region mentioned in the cover letter;

4. an Ann Ambitious who plans to use her résumé *only* for employers interested in her budget or finance experience and education. This is an example of hammering home the point very hard.

Employers like to be aware of your objective at a glance. However, a cover letter is often the better place to include such data; you would need to individualize your résumé quite a bit to write an objective that truly hits home. Plan to prepare two or three different résumés tailored to the types of employers you are targeting. Here are some examples:

A forthcoming M.U.P. graduate seeks an entry-level urban planning position, preferably in land use or transportation planning. (*Note:* this professional objective indicates direct level of job, an academic credential, and two specific areas of interest. It is precise and specific.)

Entry-level personnel position. Skills include personnel training, career development, and college recruiting. (*Note:* rather general objective, but good on emphasizing diverse skills)

Summer internship or volunteer position in an acute-care hospital or another health facility. (*Note:* a basic professional objective that indicates strong flexibility)

Summer clerkship with a Rhode Island Law firm. (very specific)

Entry-level administrative position. Desired areas/skills include: program analysis, financial management, personnel, and labor relations. (*Note:* succinct and hard-hitting, despite extremely general objective)

Avoid these typical traps in style and tone:

1. *Clichés.* "I am seeking a responsible position that will allow me to use my professional skills in a growth position."

2. *Self-centeredness:* "I am looking for a position that will enable me to use my finance skills and general business training to develop professionally."

3. *Excess verbiage.* "I am seeking a position that will enable me to develop my professional skills, round out my academic training, and gain greater insight . . ." The shorter and more specific your professional objective is, the better. If possible, use phrases rather than complete sentences.

The Summary

A summary (also at the top of your résumé) is a one or two sentence synopsis of your résumé that incorporates goals and skills.

If you have fewer than ten years of experience, it is probably foolish to write a summary. It would be preferable to use a job or career objective instead. Here is a good example, however:

> A recent Wharton MBA with five years of marketing experience in multinational enterprise seeks a position in a conglomerate.

Special Concerns

At the top of this list is the issue of falsifying information on your résumé. If you are contemplating this at all, be warned that you are likely to be caught since employers estimate that fully 20 percent of all résumés contain false data. As a result of this situation, there is far greater emphasis on reference checks and the like. If you get caught, consider the serious negative impact upon your reputation over the long haul, not to mention the likelihood of being fired immediately.

Now let's look at other issues.

If you have been fired: If you have ever been fired from a position, do not indicate it on your résumé!

Salary requirements or history: Never talk about salary on a résumé unless you wish to be ruled out by an employer who refuses to give a $30,000 salary to someone currently making $20,000 (even though you may be seriously underpaid). Although employers advertising in the classifieds often request such information, you are not obligated to provide it. If you do wish to talk money before you've even interviewed for the job, do it in your cover letter.

Controversial affiliations: Are you an activist in an anti-abortion, feminist, or radical organization? Consider your audience. One solution might be to have a "straight" and a radical résumé.

Lengthy periods of unemployment or other significant time gaps: Do not make your dates overly prominent on your résumé. They should not dominate the left-hand margin.

The best way to break up chronology is to adopt a thematic (as opposed to chronological) format.

Too many short-term positions: Be careful that a string of short-term jobs does not make you look unstable. Clearly indicate that these were temporary or summer positions. For college jobs, write, "summer 1987" instead of 6/1/87–9/1/88 or state explicitly that your position was part-time.

See "Ann Ambitious" for a way of summarizing a whole group of odd jobs succinctly.

If you have stayed too long at a job to finance graduate school: Avoid looking as if you are going nowhere. Make it clear that your employer has paid your tuition, especially if the position is a low-level one. And especially if it is a full-time position and you are a part-time student.

Should you indicate a reason for leaving jobs? In general, no, unless a succession of jobs threatens to convey an image of instability. State clearly after the job description, "Reason for leaving: grant expired."

Using a photo: This is not an accepted practice. Use your judgment to decide whether a photo will be to *your* advantage.

Common extraneous details about military service: Excessive details of army discharge or rank should not clutter your résumé. However, if your army job was pertinent to your current job goal, highlight it.

Career changers: Do not list any certifications or professional memberships in your former field. They will only make it harder for an employer to focus on your new field. Adding a professional objective to your résumé may help to reinforce your commitment to your new field. See the discussion of job or career objectives, p. 149.

The Woman Returning to Work

Make certain that your résumé begins with your degree(s) since these will probably be your primary bridge to the future job you want. Be sure that you make yourself look as professionally interesting as possible by stressing special skills, course concentration, special areas of interest, and any other category that you think will increase your market appeal. A woman with skills that are in demand in the marketplace is headed for a good job. Don't worry about making the account of your studies too long.

If you have been actively involved in community affairs, examine each civic "job" you have had for evidence of transferable skills and personal effectiveness in getting the job done.

Omit any reference to age of children or husband's name or occupation. Such homey details will reinforce the reader's image of you as a former housewife instead of a budding professional.

Take special pains to create a visually pleasing résumé to show that you know the rules of the professional game.

Ignore advice to write a functional résumé that never explicitly links the list of skills to a specific job, employer, or organization. Employers want to know the facts, not your hyperbolic subjective assessment. Only when skills are presented in a specific context do they take on the desirable "objectivity."

4

The Cover Letter

A well-written cover letter can be pivotal in an effective job campaign. Interviews can be won or lost on the basis of a résumé and cover letter as a package. An applicant with average credentials can dramatically increase interviews because of superior cover letters; a superior applicant can lose out because of poorly written or grammatically incorrect letters. In those fields where writing skills are considered critical, a résumé may only be skimmed, but a cover letter will nearly always be scrutinized. Since it is far easier to compose well-written cover letters than it is to earn the credentials for an impressive résumé, every job hunter should take pains with cover letters.

An effective cover letter can tell an employer important details about you that a résumé cannot. A good cover letter will:

1. display your writing skills and emphasize the professionalism of your approach;

2. reveal your ability to get to the point directly and incisively;

3. show that you have done your homework thoroughly about the field and/or the particular employer;

4. illustrate your awareness of those skills or training that are relevant to effective job performance;

5. communicate your motivation;

6. anticipate and address any problematic aspects of your résumé (such as lengthy periods of unemployment or an interrupted degree) that might otherwise predispose an employer unfavorably;

7. suggest a pleasing personality.

Like the advertisement that companies create to "position" their product in a competitive market, a pertinent, well-written, and professional cover letter will help to distinguish you among a crowd of other applicants, the majority of whom will typically lavish care on their résumés but treat the cover letter in a perfunctory way.

Although excerpts of both effective and ineffective cover letters are included here, no complete cover letters have been used as samples. There is an important reason for this: Intelligent professionals should learn how to write their own letters. To be sure, the first few cover letters you write may require sustained effort, but soon you will become adept at dashing them off. Eventually you will have created your own useful file of sample letters for reference.

Besides, you don't want to be one of the poor souls rejected for the reason cited in the following cautionary tale.

In preparing this book I met the chief recruiter for a company that annually hires more than 700 new professionally trained employees. He told me about a career guide he knew that featured a sample cover letter with the following opening sentence: "I know I don't have any experience, but . . ." He knew about the book because he had received 200 cover letters that began with that very sentence!

If you don't want to look foolish, write your own cover letters.

A cover letter can and should be used whenever you use your résumé. Nearly every job hunter automatically responds to a classified advertisement by attaching a cover letter to his or her résumé, or sends out a large unsolicited mailing to employers consisting of cover letters and résumés. But you should be as enterprising as you can about other possible uses. For example, you may be registered with a placement office that sends out your résumé directly to those employers whose advertisements on a bulletin board interest you. Instead of having the office send only your résumé, ask if you can add an individual cover letter. A second possibility is to attach a cover letter to employers screening your résumé during an on-campus recruitment program.

A well-written cover letter communicates to the individual employer in a direct and specific way. Never use one standard form letter for all jobs; it won't win interviews. Many employers are offended by the obvious impersonality.

There is one exception, however. If you are planning a large mailing to a group of homogeneous employers, you probably can write one letter that will serve for all. See pp. 174–75 for details.

The Elements of a Good Cover Letter

All good cover letters have common elements regardless of the specific circumstances that led to their writing and regardless of the career field. A good cover letter

1. is cast in standard business format;

2. addresses a person rather than a function;

3. identifies the desired position or type of position quite specifically or explains the circumstances that led to the letter;

4. focuses upon the writer's relevant skills, training, or experience either by highlighting the résumé or by adding information;

5. refers briefly to the résumé and any other possible enclosures;

6. requests an interview;

7. thanks the employer;

8. does not exceed one page of approximately four fairly brief paragraphs.

Address the Letter Properly

A cover letter should always be sent to a person by name and title rather than to a function. If you plan to send out a large mailing composed of unsolicited letters and résumés to employers (see pp. 174–75), finding out names is essential. Not only do employers always notice such basic good manners but many personnel directors who receive and screen thousands of unsolicited letters annually will instantly throw out letters addressed to a function. They don't have the time to consider seemingly indifferent and unmotivated applicants.

Such information is readily obtained. If the employer is local, call and ask the switchboard operator for the name of the person in charge of hiring or personnel. If the employer is out-of-state, scan basic reference tools and directories in your field. Look through information on file with your placement office or, if necessary, write the company asking for the right name of the person you want to address!

One can even be enterprising about responding to a classified ad that might list the company name but no person. For example, a recent advertisement for an "employee relations assistant" in the Boston *Globe* referred all applicants to a "J. M. Smith" at the company. Only one of the 300 people who subsequently replied bothered to call the company and ask for the full name of J. M. Smith. J. M. Smith turned out to be a Janet, who very much appreciated receiving one letter addressed to Ms. Janet M. Smith rather than Mr. J. M. Smith. Of the three people interviewed, the applicant mentioned above was the one interviewed largely on the basis of his cover letter.

What can you do about a box-number reply when you can't possibly know the name, much less the sex of the employer? Your best bet is to write to (1) Ms./Sir or (2) Miss/Sir or (3) To Whom It May Concern. It is best to avoid "Mrs." because single women may resent this form of address; the widespread use of "Ms." tends to make it the most acceptable.

Proper business format should be followed for all cover letters. Include your return address on the top right side as well as the date. Address the letter fully, including zip code:

Mr. Harvey Smith
Executive Vice President
Smith and Wells, Inc.
30 Park Avenue
New York, New York 10023

Introductory Elements

The opening paragraph of marketing/job interview letters should include the following information:

1. succinct details about your graduate and/or undergraduate degree, the date awarded, (or your class year), and the university;

2. the specific position or type of position desired;

3. any other pertinent information such as how you came to write this letter (classified advertisement or personal contact) or data that will immediately strengthen your candidacy for the position, be it mention of class rank, travel abroad, or a specific skill.

An effective opening also should strive to catch the reader's attention. In the following examples, notice the various ways the writers attempted to interest their readers.

You may be seeking a June 1988 M.B.A. who is in the top 25% of his University of Texas class, is fluent in four languages, and has had summer experience at several banks. (*Note:* This brief introduction is a virtual synopsis of the résumé. The introductory "you" catches the reader's attention.)

Your advertisement for an economics research associate in *The Chronicle of Higher Education* (May 15, 1988) greatly interests me since I am currently a Duke University Ph.D candidate in economics. (*Note:* The applicant tells how he learned of the job.)

I am currently a second year law student at Yale who is seeking a summer associate position with a medium-sized corporate commercial law firm in New York City. Several of my law professors have highly recommended your firm to me." (*Note:* This is very clear and straightforward. But compare the tame reference to Yale law professors with the more specific example below.)

Francis Barney suggested that I contact you for a possible position as an administrative assistant. I am a recent graduate of the University of Wisconsin and I have just relocated to Chicago, where I have been staying with Francis, an old friend of my father's from college." (*Note:* The writer stresses her contact for good reason. She knows it will help her to obtain an interview.)

I am a second-year M.S.W. student at Columbia University. Although I had hoped to interview with your company during your recent visit on September 29th, unfortunately the placement office did not screen my résumé favorably. I hope you will consider my application at this time." (*Note:* This paragraph explains important information that might preclude the applicant from being considered.)

As a native Vermonter I am eager to return there after my graduation in June 1988 from the University of Pittsburgh's medical school. I am seeking a fellowship position in cardiology. (*Note:* Since the applicant is seeking to relocate, identifying herself immediately as a native is highly pertinent information.)

I can offer you twenty years of outstanding business experience . . . and a brand-new law degree. I am a forthcoming J.D. from Ohio State University College of Law and am interested in a corporate commercial practice. (*Note:* The applicant's ironic wit depends upon an anticlimax.)

The Body

The body of the letter is the persuasive core. It consists of two or three well-written paragraphs that stress skills, experience, or training that make you a strong candidate for this specific job, and it refers to your résumé as well as any other attachments. Now you must convince an employer that your skills, training, and experience merit a personal interview. To do this, highlight only relevant facts about yourself that seem to predict future success. Here you can elaborate upon details merely suggested or outlined in your résumé. The body of your letter should pointedly address the employer's needs.

Fortunately, you already have a head start if you have prepared a relevant résumé according to the specific guidelines in chapter 3. You have decided which employers interest you, which skills they regard as most pertinent, and which of your special or unique strengths should be featured prominently on your résumé. This represents useful groundwork as you now consider the body of your cover letters.

It can also help to personalize the employer if you imagine a face-to-face situation where he or she is asking, "Why should I hire you?" Your cover letter should provide a partial answer, but avoid an approach that is too general. As with résumés, the "smorgasbord" approach lacks a "voice." Since a cover letter creates rapport, don't try to sell oranges, ice cream, and lettuce to someone who only wants milk.

In writing the body of the letter, any materials written or distributed by the employer, such as an annual report or a firm résumé, will be helpful. If your letter is in response to an advertisement, use the employer's own description of the ideal candidate as a way to organize your content and speak directly to the employer's concerns.

Here are some effective samples drawn from different fields and contexts.

Teaching Applicant

As the enclosed résumé indicates, I have substantive teaching experience at the college level. At Northeastern, where I was a lecturer for three years, I was the only non-Ph.D. allowed to teach senior electives and honors seminars. At Marymount, where I was subsequently an assistant professor of English, I won the Great Teacher Award for 1986.

Although I consider myself a generalist within the field of Modern British Literature, my research and publications are also on Dryden, Boswell, and eighteenth-century satire.

Notice how the second paragraph stresses the applicant's expertise and diversity. He wishes to assure his reader that he is equipped to teach courses outside his apparent specialty. His mention of "publications" is specific and more hard-hitting than merely citing an "interest." The sentence about teaching electives is a good example of a detail that is easier to convey gracefully in a letter than on a résumé.

Law Clerk

At both the Wharton School and the University of Chicago, I have concentrated my electives in the following areas:

Taxations	Securities Regulation
Corporate Law	Accounting
Estate Planning	Financial Management

In addition to this broad background, I am currently engaged in research for Rona Simmons, professor of taxation and decedents' estates. This combination of legal and nonlegal training furnishes me with a body of knowledge well suited to corporate law practice and financial planning.

It is perfectly acceptable to cite electives, especially if your résumé does not list a course concentration. Notice how the visual presentation of this data in list form makes it look important. Finally, the applicant's last sentence synthesizes the facts into a summary that is his trump card.

Business Applicant

> A copy of my résumé is enclosed. Please note that I am a member of the Harvard Business Review, a holder of a William Peabody Fellowship, and rank approximately in the top 10 percent of my class. Several faculty members have written recommendations for me, and these and a copy of my academic transcript can be forwarded to you at your request.

This applicant has stressed his faculty support because he wishes to imply strong backing. This letter is cast in a very matter-of-fact tone that is most effective with objectively impressive credentials.

Museum Administrator Applicant

> Second, I have a great deal of related experience. I have designed the curriculum for our new academic program in museum administration, served on the board of directors for the Honig Museum for ten years, and recently was awarded a $5,000 challenge grant by the Ford Foundation for developing a cooperative artists gallery at the college.

This paragraph opens with a statement that needs factual support. Notice how each supporting point in the second sentence has to emphasize the applicant's *effectiveness*. Presumably he had other experience he might have selected. The points are succinctly made and convincing.

Municipal Finance Applicant

My courses have explored both the revenue and expenditure aspects of municipal finance. "Financial Analysis of Public Organizations" provided a framework and methodology for analyzing the revenue potential of an area, its actual revenue base, and its fiscal capacity. It also introduced the fundamentals of accounting for nonprofit organizations. My work in that course culminated in a report on the financial condition of Vermont's State Government. Last semester I prepared two papers on the Urban Development Corporation. The first examined the inadequacy of the self-sufficient moral obligation bond, while the second analyzed the risks associated with the allocation of financial responsibilities among the state, local, and federal governments.

This is a good example of doing the best with what you have to offer. By emphasizing the practical aspects of her coursework, the applicant manages to make academic term papers sound relevant and professional. Had she had more substantive details to draw upon, she would have used them instead.

REFER EXPLICITLY TO YOUR RÉSUMÉ. There are many possible ways to refer to your résumé.

1. "As the enclosed résumé amplifies in greater detail, I have had seven years of experience in various phases of camp administration." This quick clause is tacked onto an important summary.

2. "To highlight pertinent data on the attached résumé. . . ." This approach is effective when you wish to use the cover letter to repeat key points on the résumé.

3. "I have enclosed a copy of my résumé." This is a perfectly acceptable and direct statement. One does not

have to link the résumé to the material of the cover letter.

If you are including other attachments, refer to them briefly: "I have enclosed a copy of my résumé and transcript."

ERRORS TO AVOID IN THE BODY OF YOUR LETTER. Here are some pointers to help you avoid common mistakes in the body of the letter.

Avoid excessive detail. Your cover letter should not be a substitution for a lengthy personal interview. As you write your letter, strive for incisiveness, and justify the presence of each word and sentence.

Employers do not have the time to wade through the kind of excessive verbiage typified in the following example:

> The shortcomings of selecting a candidate on the basis of his or her résumé alone are well known. Although mine does succeed in at least intimating in what areas my strengths may lie, it too is in need of supplementation. I have a great deal of interest in the philosophical aspects of criminal justice administration systems. As a result, I have found that attention to the theoretical and philosophical aspects of criminal justice administration is a far cry from drudgery. A proper job balance of the pragmatic and the abstract can, I believe, imbue one's job with an enviable elegance and zest.

This applicant should have used his cover letter to suggest his potential to deal with daily problems effectively rather than to reflect ambivalence toward his career choice! The former is relevant; the latter is irrelevant.

Focus upon the employer's frame of reference and values, not your own. Note the inappropriate focus on grades in the next example:

> Most satisfying to me, in my social work training, has been the realization of my interest and aptitude for research methodol-

ogy. My gratifying initial experience with a course taught by Professor Howard O'Connor led me to Professor Myron Smith's course in research design, the most difficult of all courses in the school. My success in that course, where I received the highest grade in the class and the only "A" he has awarded in the past ten years, strengthened my resolve to become a researcher.

It is possible to show academic enthusiasm and yet still reflect professional rather than student values. Note how this next applicant manages to keep the needs and concerns of the employer clearly in focus.

Ever since a Wharton course in multinational enterprise analyzing the ramifications of private international trade decisions, I have been fascinated by transnational affairs. Currently, in a class on public international law, I am writing a paper, "Tax Law for Imports." Further, I have lived and traveled abroad for an extended period of time which has left me with a heightened sense of some of the problems and considerations that might be encountered in international law.

Avoid writing an essay. While an interesting comment or two about your field is entirely justified, a lengthy paragraph may bore or annoy a busy employer. Here is an example of earnestness gone awry:

As a student of public administration and political science, my course work and subsequent research projects have dealt with the areas of societies' needs and a government's ability to respond to them, via the economic, social, or political processes. Moreover, the keener degree of awareness which has become a more integral element in today's governmental decision-making process since the 1960s has substantially widened the range of issues to which the leaders of both the public and the private sectors must address themselves. Such complexities, I believe, revolve around the conflict between "equity" and "efficiency," or the manner in which services are provided to those in most need of them, without imposing a heavy personal cost on the population as a whole. The resolution of this issue establishes the basis for responsible management; for it serves to demonstrate to citizens and to outside investors the ability of those persons in key positions to incorporate all essential ingredients in order to bring about a final product which encourages the expansion of a given area, and not its abandonment by the more productive members of the community.

The Closing

This paragraph should include the following data:

1. an explicit request for an interview, plus any information about limitations of time (or an intended visit to the employer's city if you apply out-of-state);

2. an explicit thank-you to the employer;

3. the valediction.

Since obtaining an interview is your goal, always state it explicitly: "I would welcome an opportunity for an interview at your convenience."

If there are limitations to your availability, state them directly: "I would welcome the opportunity to meet with you at a mutually convenient time. I can be available any Monday, Wednesday, or Friday that suits you."

You can thank the employer in the following ways:

> Thank you for your time and consideration.
> Thank you in advance for your consideration.
> Thanking you in advance for your consideration, I am,
>   Sincerely yours,

Acceptable closings are: "Sincerely yours" or "Yours truly," followed by your typed and handwritten signature.

The Style and Appearance of the Cover Letter

To an employer, your cover letter is the sole clue to your proficiency with the English language. Not only must your letters be grammatically and typographically *perfect* but you must also write them in an appropriate style.

1. Aim for simple but precise language. For example: "I am a forthcoming master's in electrical engineering interested in an engineering position with your company." Such virtues of simplicity were ignored in another version of this applicant's cover letter.

Having graduated from the University of Colorado with a master's in electrical engineering, I have decided to pursue a career in a company such as yours.

2. If there is a reason for your particular interest in a certain employer, say so directly and succinctly. For example: "Professor John Sears, my research adviser, has repeatedly told me of your leadership in the field of prenatal nutrition."

3. Strive for precise, specific language. Avoid trite clichés and empty phrases such as:

Employment at a highly diversified company such as yours represents a *challenging and stimulating beginning* to a career in business as well as the opportunity to significantly augment one's education.

Although I am young, I have learned a great deal about human nature. I am in search of a *meaningful growth position* where I can use my talents and skills in a *responsible, challenging way*. I am a *creative thinker*.

Avoid vague terms such as "meaningful growth opportunity" and "creative thinker." Substitute "management trainee" or another specific term for "meaningful growth opportunity" or a "responsible" or "challenging" position. It's not the employer's job to figure out what you might find challenging; he has specific jobs to fill. Tell him what you want and assess whether or not the opportunity is meaningful at the interview!

4. Be concise. The best antidote for excessive wordiness is to read over a draft of your letter with a red pen in hand. Be prepared to justify each word. Notice, for example, how only the last sentence of the following paragraph is pertinent or substantive:

I understand that your personal obligations, in combination with the huge volume of applications through which you must wade, leave you with a limited amount of time to spend on each. With this in mind, thank you for your time and consideration.

In trying to identify with the employer's burden, the applicant unwittingly took up even more of the employer's time!

5. Use the active voice. The only way to sound energetic is to use the active voice. For example, state:

"I would welcome the opportunity for an interview," not "An interview at your convenience is requested." Write, "I acquired a skill in economic analysis from these courses," not "From these courses, a skill in economic analysis was acquired."

An applicant's discomfort at actually writing a cover letter or even applying for a job can often result in excessive abruptness.

To help you hear the tone of your letter, wait a day before mailing it out, or have someone else read your letters aloud or silently.

Many professionals equate a professional style with a cool tone. The ideal cover letter, however, conveys the person behind the applicant. To create the rapport that will win you interviews, you must reveal some human warmth. Read the following example aloud to hear the tone of commanding coldness you'll need to avoid:

Contact me if you have a suitable opening.

Do not be afraid to sound enthusiastic for fear it will be misinterpreted as feigned interest by a cynical employer. Always convey your enthusiasm professionally, by anchoring it to a credential or relevant fact. For example: "As a result of my fascination with gerontology, I obtained an H.E.W. fellowship to write a dissertation on the problems of indigent elderly women."

Remember that the employer is the stranger who must be persuaded to interview you. Problems of inappropriate tone may occur if you confuse him with another group or person. For example, naïve job hunters often mistakenly perceive the employer as a career counselor or as a "buddy" with whom to share fantasies. Don't close a letter this way: "I would very much appreciate talking with you so as to obtain a clearer perspective on my career goals." It is not the employer's responsibility to counsel you. Get the advice elsewhere!

A second problem arises when applicants approach the employer in a narcissistic way. To win interviews you must convince the employer you can help him rather than vice versa, as in this unfortunate example:

Employment at a highly diversified company such as yours offers many attractive health and vacation benefits. Moreover, it gives a challenging start to one who hopes to open his own business some day.

Some applicants mistakenly regard the employer as an audience in search of entertainment. This can lead to the kind of self-conscious "cuteness" exhibited in the following example:

Is there something special about a person who graduated six months early from both high school and college and has never cut a class in her entire educational career?

If you are tempted to point to any perceived inadequacies, remind yourself that employers are not confessors. It is self-destructive to point out facts that can harm you and which might otherwise have gone unnoticed. For example:

I am a forthcoming graduate of M.I.T.'s program in electrical engineering. While I did not win any significant research prizes, I . . .

Here is how a severe case of sour grapes was transmitted in a cover letter that manages to sound both confessional and hostile at the same time:

Academically, I stand well within the top half of my class. A failure to be glib on exams prevented me from qualifying for Phi Beta Kappa. However, this failure has not prevented me from succeeding in any other endeavor.

Sometimes it will be necessary to carefully stress the positive aspects of a situation that could easily have negative connotations to an employer. One woman reentered the job market using this bad opening sentence in her cover letter:

> Seven years ago I resigned from a career in business to raise a family.

Her opening could easily have suggested an enterprising person had she thought to lead with her strengths:

> Your organization may be interested in a seasoned personnel administrator who has started her own successful business and consulted with an executive search firm concurrently with starting a family.

Do not indulge in subjective self-praise:

> The enclosed résumé sketches my background and shows my creativity, outstanding leadership skills, and writing ability.

Let the employer draw inferences from factual statements! Or if you wish to point to the clear inference, be modest and less blunt. For example:

> While still a student, I have obtained useful managerial skills through various activities. For example, my work on the student newspaper helped to sharpen my business, editorial, and writing skills. During my second summer, an administrative-assistant position in a small office helped to train me in bookkeeping procedures, employee benefits, and general office systems. Recently, as a management intern assigned to the Deputy Mayor's Office, I obtained excellent exposure to public management problems.

Here is another good example:

> During my graduate school career, I have tried to combine a seriousness of intellectual purpose with the development of interpersonal leadership skills. As chairman of the Student-Faculty Committee on Student Life, president of the student body, and senator-at-large in the university senate, I have gained useful training for a career in educational administration.

Sometimes a personality trait, such as leadership, is an important criterion of the job. If it seems important to stress such a quality do so substantively, as in the following example:

> I have learned that an effective personality is an important asset in a successful public relations career. As a result, I have tried to polish and refine my interpersonal skills through a number of special workshops on leadership styles and interpersonal effectiveness. When I received the "Outstanding Student Leader" Award at Yale last year, I felt encouraged about my own future potential to work effectively with others.

Avoid the puffery of the alternative version:

> I believe that I have the kind of sparkling personality that is essential to a successful career in public relations.

Visual Elements

A good cover letter should not exceed one page. Save the elaborate detail for the interview, when the employer is certain to be more interested. Keep the paragraphs in your letter short for the greater visual ease of your reader.

Center the letter, and allow two to four inches as a border under your signature. The letter should not look crowded. Top and side margins should be generous.

Use bond paper in $8\frac{1}{2}'' \times 11''$ size. Ideally, the paper should match that of your résumé, but if that proves too difficult, don't worry about it. Avoid corrasable paper unless you are such a poor typist that *not* using it will make it impossible for you to type letters. You might consider paying someone else to type the letter on bond for you. If at all possible, don't use an old college typewriter or a dot matrix printer for your letters.

Neatness is important. If your cover letters have obvious corrections, there may be adverse reactions. In any event you'll look unprofessional.

Proofread carefully for errors. A mispelled name, a run-on sentence, or a typographical error can easily cost you an interview! You cannot be too much of a perfectionist in this area.

If you plan to send out a hundred résumés to one specific kind of employer, convenience is important. Write one good cover letter and reproduce it on a word processor so that each one is an "original."

A Checklist

Want to write a cover letter? Sit down and fill in the blanks:

1. I am *(June graduate; M.B.A., from N.Y.U.)* _____

2. I want a job as *(a junior accountant)* _____

3. I can offer you *(skills, experience)* _____

4. I am enclosing a résumé _____

5. I want to see you *(request an interview)* _____

6. Thank you!

Now polish the language, flesh out the concepts, and you have an effective cover letter.

Guidelines for writing cover letters for networking situations are included in chapter 2. There are many instances where it is far preferable to send a letter (without the résumé) asking for an appointment on the basis of your search for advice or information than to send a résumé with a cover letter. Be certain to review the material on networking in chapter 2 so that you have all necessary factors considered.

5

The Interview

There is probably no more anxiety-provoking period in a new professional's job hunt than the interviewing stage. According to those who have survived a season of it, interviewing is that time in one's life when the threat of damp palms cancels out the pleasurable weight of a Phi Beta Kappa key, when the purchase of the first tea-and-crumpets dress in years brings on an identity crisis, and when every other candidate's brand-new pinstripe suit and waxy smile seems as frankly artificial as your own.

Such anxiety is both unproductive and avoidable, for when interviewing is undertaken in the right spirit, it can be challenging. Not only does it provide another important test of one's professional acumen but the interview reaffirms the importance of certain attributes often disregarded in the classroom. It should be a relief to many recent graduates to realize that personality, grace, tact, wit, and the ability to converse count heavily in that world in which interpersonal skills are as important to professional success as academic credentials.

Why are interviewing skills so critical? Try to get hired without having an interview first! Whereas the goal of the résumé may be to get you an interview, the goal of the interview is to get you the offer. Of the two, the latter is the far more complex task. Many people can put together a well-organized, attractive résumé, but it is rarer to find inexperienced professionals who can interview well on the first try.

All too often, for example, new professionals tend to regard an interview as a social rather than a strategic conversation. Although they unfailingly prepare for term papers and tests by doing diligent research, they approach an interview with the casualness and spontaneity reserved for an encounter with an old friend. They forget to research the organization, agency, or firm with which they are having the interview. They forget to prepare questions in advance. They forget to develop an effective strategy to market themselves successfully. They forget to analyze their weaknesses to prepare for difficult or probing interview questions. In brief, they fail to do the kind of planning that can make the difference between success and failure. As a result, they appear unmotivated, disorganized, unprepared. There is no magic to interviewing. It is a skill that can be learned, but like any other skill, it takes determination, care, practice, and coaching.

What follows is a commonsense guide to the interview

marathon. Aimed at the inexperienced job hunter, it is a compendium of practical suggestions and tips that placement directors, career counselors, and experienced recruiters all find themselves sharing. First become familiar with the psychology of the interview. There, the all-important principles are laid out for you. If you keep these truths clearly in mind, you should be able to adapt easily to the demands of any specific employment situation, even when the unexpected occurs. The specific examples, drawn from a variety of professions, are equally adaptable to your particular circumstances, for although the outward trappings of the interview format may vary considerably from profession to profession, interview skills are transferable.

The next section of the chapter helps you to develop your interview strategy and includes a quiz on weaknesses, a sampling of questions to ask (and not to ask directly), and guidelines for creating an effective interview strategy. Also included is a summary of an effective interview by a young woman named Sally Savvy.

The final section, the "Interview Savvy" test, asks you to choose among answers to some difficult interview problems and then comments on each possible answer.

The Psychology of the Interview

No One Is Hired on Merit Alone

The interview is *not* an objective process in which the employer selects the best candidate, but a highly subjective encounter where he is evaluating whether he likes you enough as a person to associate with you professionally for eight or more hours per day.

So, first and foremost, recognize that personality, presence, and enthusiasm count for a lot. Although most employers will readily admit how difficult it is to evaluate someone's personality fairly on the basis of a thirty-minute or one-hour interview, when the time comes to decide who should be offered the job or even invited back for a second or third interview, recruiters invariably choose the candidates they liked the best. Even if employers openly state their hiring criteria in advance and interview only those people who fit their "objective" standards, after that the selection process invariably centers on chemistry. As with blind dates, so too with interviewing: first impressions are decisive.

Can you identify the elements that cause an employer to like you? Not really, alas, for employers are as subject as the rest of us to individual preferences. Yet we all can think of people who make a strong positive impression on those around them. Generally they are warm, outgoing, enthusiastic, and positive about life. They are self-confident, responsive, and considerate. Instead of trembling at the thought of being judged by an interviewer, they regard the interview as an opportunity to learn more about a firm or organization, to investigate a possible exciting opportunity, or to sharpen their conversational skills. Even if they have no other current job offers, they manage not to feel desperate or unduly anxious. As a result, during an interview, they seldom project nervousness, timidity, or anxiety.

You can be encouraged by their example if you note that your task is not to acquire an entirely new personality but rather to release existing interpersonal skills to meet the demands of a professional situation.

The Interviewer Is under Stress

Very few job hunters realize how stressful it can be for employers to conduct an interview. Unless they are in personnel, the chances are that they have little on-the-job experience at interviewing prospective employees. Consider the amount of time that must go into finding a suitable person to fill a job opening, and then think of a harassed or very active boss having to fit that amount of time into an already busy schedule.

Most employers are not confident of their interviewing skills and readily admit that they find instant assessments a problem. They can be shy about asking probing interview questions that make applicants uncomfortable. Moreover, because they do tend to hire the people they like best, they are extremely susceptible to choosing a candidate who is not subsequently as charming or pleasant as in the interview. In brief, employers can be fooled.

Employers also fear that superiors and colleagues will ultimately blame them for any hiring mistakes. You can imagine, then, the employer's relief when an applicant walks in the door with a manner so reassuringly professional, a poise so clearly impressive, and a personality so distinctly appealing that the decision to hire is instinctive and easy. Above all, employers want to feel self-confident about their hiring decisions.

Thus confidence is the key during an interview. In some instances it will be up to you to set the employer at ease, to ask most of the questions, to compensate for his conversational deficiencies, and generally to alleviate his discomfort. If you want the job, you will have to take subtle control of the situation. Such control will be relatively easy provided that you have done thorough homework and project self-assurance.

You Must Play an Active Interview Role

One of the most frequent employer complaints is that inexperienced graduates are too passive during the interview.

Many job hunters simply play an answering role, leaving the employer to take the initiative. But the candidate who talks and interacts gets the job, not the person who is withdrawn and monosyllabic. Ideally, an interview is a strategic conversation. It should not be an interrogation, a mere oral review of a résumé, or a tedious exchange of factual information.

The Best Interviews Are Conversations

Interviews are conversations with a purpose. The goal toward which you should be striving is to make your conversation not only pertinent but dynamic. Think of your job interviews as verbal tennis games: not only should you return the conversational cues of the employer but you should serve some of your own. For example, when an employer asks, "What are you looking for in a job?" you might answer the question and then add, "What are you looking for in an employee?" When he answers, you might point out how you think you fill the bill. Of course you can't say that you are smart, wonderful, and the world's most winning personality. However, by all means point to facts that show your assets.

Then let's say the employer notices something specific on your résumé, such as your having been brought up in Nebraska. Pick up this conversational lead. Ask him if he has ever visited there. Anything is preferable to merely nodding or murmuring, "Yes, I am from Nebraska." Your response to a trivial conversational cue may not get you the job, but it could certainly help to warm up a lifeless interview. Like it or not, in order to obtain job offers you will not only have to talk well but also initiate dialogue throughout.

Dynamic conversation gives you a chance to show how articulate, fast-thinking, and intelligent you are. Talking well is an indispensable professional skill.

How much talking should you do? Ideally, about 40 percent. The most skillful interviewers will get you to talk. Similarly, the most skillful applicants will spur the employer to talk. To achieve this, however, you will need to ask probing questions about the company operation, the career field in general, or the specific job requirements.

To win offers, your interview must challenge and stimulate rather than bore the employer. By taking an active lead in the conversation, you can help prevent it from being an interrogation, a boring and utterly predictable monologue, or a stiff encounter.

Some sample interview questions appear on pp. 193–98.

Appear Confident

Projecting an image of self-confidence is important because part of the job under consideration may consist in being poised with high-ranking people. If you are nervous or awed during the interview, the employer will assume you will act similarly with an important client.

To be sure, a job interview can be fairly intimidating, but your ability to act comfortable will suggest an ability to stand up well under equally intimidating job pressures. "Thinking on your feet" describes the desirable combination of flexibility and cool assurance that successful professionals display in stress situations.

Projecting self-confidence also increases the employer's assurance that he or she has made the right hiring choice. The kind of self-confidence we are discussing is more subtle than "I'd love the job" or "I'll do a very good job." Such statements always backfire because they suggest anxiety or desperation. Instead, self-confidence means a steady assurance that you are more than adequate for the job and have other options and choices. Perceptive questioning during an interview helps to reveal you as the best candidate and is moreover proof positive of the kind of discriminating cast of mind typical of people with choices. Just make certain that you observe the fine line between bountiful self-confidence and inadvertent arrogance.

Prior to any interview, then, you should concentrate on bolstering your feelings of self-confidence. Stand in front of a mirror and recite out loud all of your strong points for this particular job, ranging from the courses you have taken to the ideas you have about how the job might be done. Repeat all the praise you may have received from professors or employers for work completed in the past. Be prepared for the interview by doing advance homework.

Do Your Homework

Thorough interview homework involves a number of factors.

1. Inform yourself as much as possible about the organization, agency, or firm. If possible talk to people who work there, read the firm's public relations materials, check any newspaper or magazine stories about them—in brief, research the organization as thoroughly as you researched any term paper.

2. Think through what you can do for the organization and what particular experience, skills, or abilities you should emphasize. Look over your résumé to make certain that it reflects your strengths for this particular job, and if need be, redo it to tailor it for this specific position. Even if the employer already has a copy of your résumé, carry the new one to the interview, and say you've reorganized it for greater effectiveness. Even if

the interviewer doesn't refer to it during the interview, it will be there for later reference.

3. Analyze your weaknesses so that you won't be caught off guard by a trick question such as "What is your major weakness?" A thoughtful analysis of your position may also help you to initiate an important question. If, for example, you are a Los Angeles native seeking a job in a small town, be aware of the uneasy relation that exists between city and country mouse. Small-town inhabitants are likely to think, "Why does this person want to live here?" You might explain your reasons even if the interviewer doesn't bring up the question.

4. Prepare a few good questions. These questions may help establish you as the most likely candidate for the job faster than anything else you say and do. Having questions to ask an interviewer will help you to feel and act more self-confident.

5. Arrange a mock interview beforehand. If possible, find a professional who has done some hiring in the past. Ask this person to help you analyze the forthcoming situation, get practice, and hear constructive criticism.

Criticism, in fact, is essential for improvement. Unfortunately, even though you may interview for a hundred jobs, you seldom learn your failings. You might repeat the same destructive mannerism in every interview without ever learning that twirling your hair constantly led to your downfall.

The Interview May Not Lead to a Job

Certain kinds of interviews will rarely result in job offers. Be careful not to have false expectations.

The interview that you obtain through personal influence is unpromising. Your important Uncle Henry may succeed in getting you interviews with two employers in your field who will be more than glad to talk with "Henry's nephew." You may get some useful advice from these pleasant chats, but don't expect to get an offer unless there is a specific job opening for which you are eminently well-qualified. One obvious exception is when your Uncle Henry *does* have the power to actually land you offers with people eager to please him.

A second kind of pseudo-interview may occur if your placement office allows you to sign up for an on-campus interview with any employer who interests you without pre-screening your qualifications. In such cases, the recruiter will talk pleasantly with you, but unless your credentials measure up to predetermined hiring criteria, forget about landing an offer.

A third type of interview is for a job that has secretly been filled. The employer may be forced to interview widely to comply with affirmative action requirements, but the interview will be a charade. Women and minorities should be particularly alert to this kind of interview.

Preparing for a Successful Interview

Create a Defensive Strategy

An examination of possible problems relating to your background and credentials will go a long way toward helping you anticipate adverse employer reactions. Nearly every inexperienced applicant worries about the disadvantage of inexperience at interview time. But there may be more individual aspects of your candidacy that would attract the attention of an employer, such as taking five years to complete a four-year degree.

Checklist

Answering the following list of questions should help you begin to see yourself from the employer's point of view. Answer each question honestly, and then read through the commentary that follows the questions. It explains how the employer is likely to view your answer and gives you specific pointers.

Check with a pencil any questions that seem to apply to you. Go through this list quickly and do not dwell on any particular item.

_____1.   Are you older than those typically applying for your level of position?

_____2.   Was your academic record less than $A-$?

_____3.   Did it take you longer than the norm to finish either undergraduate or graduate school? (Reasons for doing so are irrelevant at this point.)

_____4.   Do you lack substantive experience in the career area for which you are interviewing?

_____5.   Are you currently trying to change careers?

_____6.   Have you ever been fired?

_____7.   Have you changed jobs with great frequency?

_____8.   Are you foreign-born?

_____9.   Are you applying for jobs in geographical areas where you have never previously resided?

_____10.   Are you a woman applying for jobs in a male-dominated profession?

_____11.   Are you a minority professional?

_____12.   Have you had to struggle financially to obtain an education?

_____13. Have you been looking for a job for more than two or three months?

_____14. Are you without any kind of full-time professional experience (excluding summer positions)?

_____15. Do you have difficulty writing term papers, or do you always do better on exams than on papers?

_____16. Does your résumé show an undergraduate activity, such as a premedical or prelaw club, that represents a different career direction from your current aspirations?

_____17. If you worked full-time, was it ever for less than a year?

_____18. Are you a new arrival in the area where you are seeking a job?

_____19. Put a check if you have never joined a professional organization in your career field.

_____20. Check if you have not been active in any student affairs during school.

_____21. Is there anything on your résumé that suggests you are not able to relocate or travel?

_____22. Do you have any physical handicaps that are indicated on your résumé?

_____23. Are you a single or divorced woman with children?

_____24. Are you a single male over thirty who has never been married?

_____25. Were all your summer jobs either menial or in family-related concerns?

_____26. Have you changed jobs with considerable frequency but without advances in status or responsibility?

_____27. Have you worked in an organization for more than five years without a promotion?

_____28. Does your résumé state a job objective that is different from the jobs for which you have been interviewing?

_____29.   Do you live a considerable distance from the typical location of jobs where you have been applying?

If you have checked several items, or even many items, that only indicates that you are unique and individual. The point of this checklist is not to undermine your professional or personal self-confidence but rather to help you come to grips with facts and attitudes that can adversely affect your job-hunting success. The following comments about each checklist item should help you prepare for an interview defensively.

1.   The employer may think that you will be unable to take orders from a higher-ranking but younger person. He may also fear that you will have unrealistic expectations about the level of responsibility you can assume in the job. Be prepared to bring this up voluntarily to allay his anxieties.

2.   If your record is not academically distinguished, some employers will eliminate you on those grounds alone. Even if they like you, they'll have trouble defending a hiring decision about a candidate who falls below the usual standards. Be prepared to supply other pertinent evidence, such as writing samples, if you want to be considered.

3.   Employers will interpret slow progress toward a degree as weak professional motivation. This is especially true for career changers. If there were extenuating factors such as a serious illness, discuss this during the interview.

4.   Chapter 3 dwells at length on ways to present and highlight any relevant volunteer, part-time, or summer work. This can help greatly.

5.   Career changers are not easily understood by older employers. Once again, your résumé is the key to a successful presentation of your new identity. See the specific material relating to career changers. Be ready for the interview ques-

tion, "Why did you leave teaching (or whatever)?" Your answer must stress your motivation in your second career rather than your attachment to or nostalgia for the first.

6.   Few new professionals have yet had the opportunity to be fired. Career changers who may have been fired just before they started a new degree program have a ready-made explanation, so long as the employer will support their version of the facts in any reference check.

Even more important, however, is to take a close look at your résumé to see why suspicion has been aroused. Never put down on a résumé that you were fired. And if you were fired because a grant expired, say so.

7.   If you have had many jobs, an employer will quite naturally think that you are either unstable, unmotivated, or have been fired. If the changes do not suggest a pattern of advancement, be prepared to explain this disconcerting pattern. Also change your résumé so that the part-time or temporary nature of any student jobs is clearly indicated.

8.   If you are foreign-born or have a foreign-sounding name, you may encounter substantial prejudice; this depends largely upon the region. Mention U.S. citizenship, permanent resident status, or your fluency in English. See the extensive discussion of personal data in chapter 3. Many employers will be uncertain about your eligibility for work. If you have received all your schooling in the United States, there is no reason to indicate your foreign birth. Leave it for the interview.

9.   Invariably, employers will want to know why you are interested in relocating. Your cover letter should establish your motivation. Be prepared to discuss your reasons for relocating.

10.   Older male employers may still be uncomfortable in an interview with a female candidate. Your best preparation

is to gather up your self-confidence so that you'll have the poise necessary to set him at ease. Your questions and answers should reflect thorough homework and help to direct the interview into substantive areas where you can both relax and forget about sexual differences. Recognize too that the interviewer's own nervousness may cause unintentional bloopers such as calling women "girls." Judge each situation separately as you determine whether you have the character and personality to be a trailblazer or token employee. If you are extremely uncomfortable with any given employer, find out if he will be your supervisor. If not, ask to meet that person before you reject the company outright.

11.   Minority professionals being interviewed by non-minority employers should take special pains to display the kind of self-confidence that puts the interviewer at ease. Some early initiative in asking substantive questions about the job or field may help to get the conversation on a surer footing. And take advantage of the specific suggestions of another student who has been successful in obtaining offers.

12.   Most employers are impressed with any evidence of strong ambition or motivation. But don't project bitterness: "Yes, unlike most of my classmates at Princeton, I had to work my way through school." And avoid self-congratulation: "Yes, I sure had to struggle to reach my goal. But I made it with flying colors." If you are interviewing with an organization known for conservatism or even snobbery, be realistic about whether you easily fit their image. Even before you open your mouth, the wrong kind of clothing may have sealed your fate.

13.   Since employers like to think that they are hiring a candidate equally attractive to other employers, it's none of their business that you may have had some difficulty in obtaining job offers. Be as positive as possible about your situa-

tion, and imply that you are being very discriminating about accepting the right offer. Even the slightest reference to a frustrating job search may weaken your position.

14. A lack of professional experience often shows up in a disconcerting ignorance and lack of realism about a particular job or the working world in general. It is doubly important that you obtain interview practice in advance of any expected interviews, find out what constitutes appropriate dress for your specific field, and do thorough interview homework.

15. If the field demands good writing skills, try to improve fast! During the interview the employer may request a writing sample or ask, "Do you write well?" If so, don't exaggerate the seriousness of the issue. (You may be overly perfectionist.) Don't volunteer the information that you have always done better on exams.

16. If you have included a red flag about your former career aspirations on your résumé, remove it immediately. Every employer wants to think that he is hiring someone highly motivated. Be especially careful if your original aspiration was to enter a field with higher social status.

17. Leaving a job before a year without going directly to another job may cause a question in the mind of an employer, who may rightly wonder about your stability.

18. Recent relocation can easily cause you to *appear* unstable. Make certain that your résumé reflects your new address and telephone number (or at least a message number). During the interview, avoid talking about personal matters such as the difficulty of finding an apartment. You must appear to be in control of the situation, even if you don't feel that you are.

19. Your lack of interest in professional organizations may be interpreted by an employer negatively if you are a

career changer who has many other professional organizations in your former field listed.

20.   As silly as it may seem to you, extracurricular activities can help to suggest an all-around personality or leadership traits. If possible, expand your activities immediately.

21.   Ask yourself why you are applying for jobs that may require relocation or extensive travel if you are in fact unwilling to move around. If the employer asks you pointed questions, have answers prepared. For example, a woman with small children might say, "If I am offered the job and accept it, my husband can easily be an evening baby-sitter for any evenings I might want to stay late."

22.   If your handicap does not interfere with effective performance, it should never be on your résumé.

23.   If you are a divorced woman with children, omit such information from your résumé.

24.   In conservative areas of the country, a single male over thirty is likely to be suspected of homosexuality. You should be aware that inquiries about your social life may be attempts to ascertain your sexual preference. It's up to you, in either case, to decide whether to go beyond the questions that are asked. The point is to plan ahead how you will react to such inquiries.

25.   See Chapter 3 for what to do with all those jobs that do not add up to relevant experience and should not be featured prominently on your résumé. The sample résumé of Ann Ambitious offers one approach.

26.   Frequent job changes may give the impression to an employer that you are unstable. Refer to chapter 3 for information on how to rearrange chronology to emphasize the positive. Make certain that your résumé clearly indicates which jobs were part-time or temporary. And don't make dates overly prominent on your résumé.

27.   If you have never been promoted, someone may con-

clude that you are a mediocre performer, particularly if you have worked in a large organization where others are regularly promoted. If you have been working for an organization that has experienced financial setbacks, you have a ready-made rationale.

28.   An irrelevant professional objective will make you look very foolish, desperate, or stupid. If you do have a restricted objective that you want to list prominently on your résumé, do not send it for jobs that are not on target. Have two résumés.

29.   If you live a considerable commuting distance from where you have applied to work, an employer may want you to relocate or may assume that overtime work will be a problem for you. State your willingness to work overtime.

Sample Interview Questions

Now that you have prepared for the psychology of the interview, consider specific interview questions. Knowing which questions to ask and how to ask them can be the key to a good interview.

Good interview questions can be prepared in advance. Intelligent questions indicate that you are motivated enough to have done your homework; that you are articulate and intelligent; that you are organized and well-prepared; that you are self-confident and assertive; that you are thoughtful and analytic, and that you have the poise and maturity to conduct an interesting and lively discussion.

Good questions tend to be open-ended. They are critical and require thoughtful or analytical answers from the employer. These answers will be revealing about the job, the employer, or the organization.

Before going on any interview, review the following material and select the questions that seem most appropriate. Be careful how you use them. These sample questions may not all be equally useful starting points.

Training

Some entry-level professional positions automatically involve a formal training process. You may, for example, be systematically rotated through departments for six months and then be "hired" by a specific division. This is true of large retailing, accounting, and law firms. You might ask:

1. Can you tell me more about your system of training?

2. Will I systematically or informally be rotated through individual departments? If so, how many departments? How long will I stay in each?

3. Can I choose, or will I be assigned to specific departments?

4. Which departments or divisions do you feel are most critical for my professional development and advancement? Why?

5. As I rotate, what criteria will be used to gauge my progress and performance? For example, will reports be filed on me? Will I be told how I am doing, or will these reports be confidential?

6. How long will this formal or informal training last?

7. Can you describe the process whereby I am assigned to a particular "job" in your organization or firm? Does someone from a division request me? Do I have a say in where I end up? Can I say no with impunity?

8. What do you perceive to be the strengths of your training program?

9. How many people will be in the training program with me? Will we all work independently, or will there be some opportunity for group interaction?

Supervision

Understand more about this important area before you accept a job with a particular organization. If, for example, you find it difficult to work without close supervision, you ought to find out whether you will get it. You might ask:

1. How closely will I be supervised either in the training program [if applicable] or in a particular position? Will I have more than one supervisor?

2. Is there some clear progression in the degree of responsibility I will be allowed? Can you explain it?

3. To what extent will I be working independently or as a team member?

4. How much responsibility can I realistically hope to obtain in this position?

Atmosphere of the Organization

A good source of interesting interview material can be found here. These questions will help you to draw out the employer and will tell you a great deal about the organization. In fact, if the employer is at all interested in you, he or she will typically wind up making something of a sales pitch.

1. How would you describe the atmosphere? What is unique about it?

2. In your opinion, why is it a good place to work?

3. What, if any, are its weaknesses as a place to work?

4. How does it compare with X firm, agency, etc.?

Criteria for Hiring

Some applicants may find it hard to believe that you can ask an employer about his or her criteria for hiring, but indeed you both can and should. For one thing, the employer will provide you with a great deal of useful information that you can then use to sell yourself. For another, you'll find out quickly if you are in the right place. Ask about criteria for hiring and your interview will automatically become more meaningful. In fact #1 is an excellent interview opener.

1. Ideally, what kind of associate, trainee, _____ [fill in the blank to describe this particular job] are you looking for?

2. Is there anything in my résumé or background that you feel is problematic? If so, I'd like to discuss it with you. [This shows self-confidence and forthrightness.]

Substantive Questions

Generally, the brighter the applicant, the more substantive the interview will become. But it is impossible to ask substantive questions unless you have done your homework. If at all possible, familiarize yourself in advance by talking to knowledgeable staffers, ex-staffers, professors, or placement officers at your schools. Gain insight into the personalities, politics, and problems of the organization. If this is not possible, then do your reading very thoroughly to prepare. Try to approach the interview with questions such as these:

1. Is your firm still heavily involved in the Smith-Brown affair? [Make certain that you are thoroughly familiar with the issue and can discuss it well.]

2. I read in *Fortune* that you have been having serious trouble with your foreign markets. Was the article accurate? I'm curious as to how you people reacted to the article. What was the feeling about it?

3. What reaction, if any, do you see in your company because of the recent legislation in X area?

4. Some people say that the future of your industry [legal practice, retailing operation] is dependent upon _____. Do you agree with it?

5. Are there any immediate plans for expansion in your organization, either in new offices, new market areas, or new fields? In what directions are you moving?

6. How are you responding to the problem of _____? [latest trend, competition, etc.]

Questions That Should Not Be Asked Directly

Learning the rules of the working world means learning how to ask delicate questions with the requisite tact and discretion. For example, questions about salary, morale, and benefits pose complicated issues that must be approached with great caution. For some people, simply realizing that there can be two different ways to ask the same questions—right and wrong—can be an important breakthrough, both personally and professionally. Often it is not *what* you ask but *how* you ask it that matters.

Salary

Let's assume that the salary is unknown to you at the time of the interview. If so, questions about salary or salary range during an initial interview are inappropriate and premature, unless you are interviewing with a large organization that is planning to hire several people simultaneously, or an organization with a well-known training program. In such cases, the salary range is usually well known, and there is no harm in asking. But if you are in doubt as to the appropriateness of asking, don't ask.

The time to talk about money is after you have been offered the job and a specific salary. Then you have real bargaining power. (Before then, by the way, you are not obliged to tell the employer your current salary or your salary expectations.)

Vacations and Other Benefits

You'll be starting off on the wrong foot if you are direct about your vacation or other benefits. Anything that makes you look more interested in the benefits of the job than in the job itself makes you appear unmotivated.

No one is saying that you shouldn't care about benefits (retirement plans, sick leave, health insurance, maternity leave), but these are secondary considerations. Once you obtain the offer, you can ask anything you like. If you feel strongly that you want the cards on the table at an earlier stage, then say, "I am unclear about the benefits that go with this position. Could you elaborate upon them?" Such a general query is much better than a naively specific one: "How much vacation time do I get?" The hallmark of the unmotivated or naive worker is the obvious concern about benefits.

Overtime

It is perfectly natural to wonder "How hard will I have to work?" In some fields, such as retailing or law, the reputation for long hours is legendary. Even assuming that you are an extremely ambitious professional who expects to work very hard, you may worry about what the employer expects from you. In contrast, let's assume that you are concerned with finding a 9 to 5 job and wouldn't dream of getting into a situation where long hours are required. Try to schedule your interview for late afternoon. Then you'll see how busy the place is after 5 P.M. During your interview, casually ask, "What is it like to work here?" If you are lucky, the interviewer will answer, "Oh, it's very interesting, but it's a real sweatshop."

Do not, under any circumstances, succumb to the illusion that younger members of the organization who take you to lunch during a day-long interview are your "pals." They have been asked to look you over—don't make the mistake of being candid with them. Later they will feel no loyalty toward you and may, in fact, veto an offer that might otherwise have come your way.

Morale

Of course, you can't help wondering what the atmosphere is really like in an organization. But how do you cut through the public relations veneer when you are an outsider? How do you, for example, find out that Bill Smith, your intended supervisor, is really tyrannical rather than relaxed?

First of all, rely upon your instinctive reaction to the people you meet. Second, ask to be introduced to those co-workers with whom you would be associating if you got the job. If possible, try to have a few minutes of private conversation with each and ask them, "What do you think are the good points (and the bad points) of being an employee in this organization?" It's a perfectly fair question to ask, and you should learn from their replies. Possibly you'll prefer to save the introductions until after the offer is made or until you have a second interview.

Feel free to ask what happened to the last person who filled the position. Was he or she fired or promoted? If the person resigned, why? This legitimate question should give you some important clues.

After you have taken the preceding steps, sit down and review what you have heard. Did anyone, for example, say, "This is a really good place to work." Did they sound enthusiastic when they said it? Did anyone say, "Your future boss is one of the best persons to work for that I have ever known"? Look out for examples of damning with faint praise, or a conspicuous absence of enthusiasm.

One final point. Don't expect an employer to be candid in revealing the weaknesses of the job or organization. Don't be naive enough to believe all the glowing enthusiasm you hear. Remember, that just as you'll be highlighting the positive, so will they. Like it or not, you'll both be selling.

Promotions

There is an appropriate way to ask about promotions. Just say, "If I perform well in this position, what would the future hold for me?" or "What would be the next step on the ladder if I perform well in this position?" You should not be afraid to ask, but take care to avoid sounding as if your eye is directed to the second rung on the ladder rather than the first. Whatever you do, don't deprecate the value of the job for which you are interviewing.

If the next step is a clear-cut one—from law associate to partner, from deputy director to director—then obviously you will have to phrase the question differently. You might say, "How long does it generally take to be considered for partnership?" If the next rung of the ladder is already occupied by someone else, be delicate. At the time of the interview there may be a tacit understanding that the job goes nowhere—you will have to leave the organization in order to advance. If so, you won't be talking about promotions. On the other hand, if you are uncertain about the chances of moving up within the organization, zero in on this issue before you accept the job. It may be wiser to be silent, though, if you suspect that in two years you'll be substantially more marketable anyway, and your present goal is to get an immediate offer.

Keep in mind that if the position is a dead-end one, the employer is apt to be defensive or prefer to hire someone too timid to ask tough questions or too desperate to care. In the final analysis, you'll have to judge the situation on its own merits rather than proceed from abstractions.

Raises

Ask about raises in a straightforward way: "How often are raises awarded?" "Are raises fixed or set in any way?" You may also wish to ask about bonuses. Make sure you find out who has the authority to set raises and bonuses.

Now that you've thought about delicate issues, let's move on to specific problems that may occur.

Some Common Interview Problems

When the Interviewer Doesn't Know How to Interview

Many employers feel so uncomfortable interviewing that they begin the conversation with, "Well, I really don't know what to ask you." If this happens to you, here is a perfect opportunity to seize the conversational reins. No one could criticize you for being too aggressive. If the employer gives you such an easy opening, take it and don't think twice.

Move in to fill the vacuum: "Tell me what kind of candidate you are looking for." That will get the employer talking—or stumbling—and give you a great deal of information to direct you when you talk about yourself.

When the Interviewer Is Someone You Know Personally

It doesn't matter. Be prepared. Do your homework, prepare a strategy, and plan to ask substantive and probing questions.

Above all, avoid acting too breezy and wandering into excessive small talk. Avoid acting as if you are guaranteed the job. Remember, despite any pull your friend/interviewer might have, your best strategy is to ignore the connection and concentrate on showing yourself to be the best candidate.

When the Interviewer Starts Talking about Personal Problems

Surprisingly, many employers will talk candidly about their personal problems, especially if a controversial issue arises in the course of the conversation. If, for example, your résumé reveals that you are a feminist, the male employer who is currently having problems with his wife might try to learn your views. You may find yourself launched on a dangerous course when a professional interview threatens to descend into personal depths.

Why is such personal discussion so dangerous? It is out of place, first of all—an interview is not intended to be a social conversation. It is a discussion with a purpose, and the purpose is to get you a good job. Although the interviewer might enjoy talking with a stranger about personal problems, afterward he will invariably feel uncomfortable, foolish, or just plain embarrassed and will hire someone else to whom he hasn't foolishly unburdened himself.

So if the conversation gets personal, assert yourself as soon as possible. If necessary, break in and say, "This is a fascinating topic, but since time is limited, I do have some questions about the job that I'd like to ask you." The employer won't be sorry—especially in retrospect—that the conversation returned to professional matters.

When the Interviewer Wants to Talk about Your Personal Difficulties

If you have been job hunting for some time or if the job market is difficult in your particular field, very often the conversation will begin with the employer saying sympathetically, "Gee, it must be tough to be looking for a job these days." Or, "Do you know that we have had more than 400 responses to our advertisement for this position? The job market must be brutal these days."

Whatever you do, don't fall for this sympathy trap and launch into a tale of your troubles. Naive job hunters frequently respond to such an opening by agreeing, "It sure is tough to find a job when you don't have any experience. I have been looking for eight months now, and I am feeling quite discouraged." A response like this kills your chances; no one wants to hire a loser. If you have been having trouble, it's no one's business but your own. Anyone—and that includes professional friends—who is in a position to help you will be less inclined to do so if you exude failure, depression, or anxiety about your prospects. Keep your perfectly normal feelings of discouragement to yourself. Be positive when discussing your job search with an employer; imply that you are being very careful about which job offer you accept because you know how important a decision it is. Say that, yes, your classmates are finding it tough, but you feel you have been lucky. You've had some good experiences. Remember, when an employer expresses sympathy, the conversation has shifted into the domain of the personal, which should be reserved exclusively for those who love or care about you.

Many other kinds of personal issues can come up. Suffice it to say that you must be discreet about what topics you are willing to discuss with a perfect stranger who is sitting there judging you. Of course, you can talk about yourself personally if it seems relevant—your summer in France, your childhood on a farm, your paper route. These are safe topics. Use your judgment and refrain from discussing your divorce, your childcare problems, and so on.

When the Interviewer Begins by Looking at Your Résumé

Since most people will read a page from top to bottom, the entries at the top of your résumé should be highly relevant.

Don't begin your résumé with your high school education; if possible, begin it either with your professional education or your professional experience. You might also begin it with a professional objective. (See chapter 3).

Often between the time you apply for a particular job and obtain an actual interview, you realize that you could prepare a much more pertinent résumé. Do so and bring it to the interview. If you can, give it to the employer at the very start, especially if he or she takes out your résumé and is obviously looking it over. Just say, "I brought along a better résumé for you. It highlights my exact experience in. . . ."

When You Have a Special Physical Handicap or Personal Belief That Will Restrict Your Job Performance

It is very important to bring up special job-related problems during an interview. Orthodox Jews, for example, who are strict Sabbath observers should inform the employer that they will not be able to work Friday evenings or Saturdays if it appears likely that this will be part of the job. But mention this at the *end* of the interview, after you have had the opportunity to sell yourself.

Similarly, if you have a heart ailment that will prevent your maintaining a strenuous physical pace, bring it up if you think it is relevant. Make certain the employer knows that it will not interfere with your job performance.

Now that you are well versed in the preparatory elements of an effective interview, read about an ideal interview. Sally Savvy's experiences can serve as a useful interview checklist.

A Day in the Life of an Interviewee

Before the Interview

1. Sally looks over her résumé. She may revise it for this particular employer.

2. She puts an extra copy of her résumé in her briefcase, just in case the employer has misplaced his copy.

3. She collects other materials, such as memos from previous jobs, transcripts, letters of recommendation—whatever might be helpful. She'll use these if it seems appropriate at the time.

5. She finds out how to get to her interview and allows time for getting lost if the location is unfamiliar. She also jots down the name and telephone number of the interviewer in case she should become unavoidably detained.

6. She doesn't box herself in with another appointment an hour later. She keeps a bloc of hours clear. After all, the employer may be running late, especially if there are multiple interviews scheduled.

7. She has jotted down some good questions to ask. She may review them in the ladies' room just before the interview begins but has no intention of referring to written notes during the actual interview.

8. She has reviewed her strengths for this particular job. She knows what she has to offer and plans to steer the conversation gracefully toward these selling points.

9. She knows her weaknesses equally well. At a midpoint in the conversation she may interject, "Is there anything

in my background that you consider problematic?" If she is lucky, the employer will deal with reservations candidly, and she'll have a chance to explain or deemphasize them.

10. Her clothing expresses conservative professional elegance. Although she tries to look her most attractive, there is nothing seductive about her appearance—no heavy perfume, plunging neckline, or heavy makeup. If she is unsure how to dress, she asks the advice of a successful professional woman.

11. In the reception room, Sally is polite and gracious to the receptionist at the front desk, the employer's secretary, and everyone else she meets along the way. She's shrewd enough to know how often a discerning boss asks the staff for candid reactions to a candidate.

12. She has come prepared for delay, knowing that other people are being interviewed, that the employer is a busy person, that interviews seldom start on time. Perhaps she purposely chats pleasantly with the secretary for a few minutes.

13. She has arrived a good ten minutes early, because the last time she went for an interview she was twenty minutes late and the employer was obviously annoyed even after she apologized. She ended up offering to reschedule her appointment.

The Interview

1. Sally extends her hand to the employer automatically. This establishes her professionalism, especially if the employer has not offered his or her hand. Her palms are dry, her handshake firm.

2. Even though she smiles warmly during the introductory moments, she avoids using the employer's first name unless specifically encouraged to do so.

3. If the employer's office is attractive, she may "spontaneously" react to it with a compliment during the first minute or two. "What a lovely painting" or "I like your Chagall (or whatever)". She recognizes that during the first few moments such a remark is perfectly appropriate. It will make her seem relaxed, if she has some personal comment, for the interview proper has not yet begun. If the interview is on her campus, she makes a small joke about the office they have given to the employer. Whatever seems like a human, personal, or genial remark is perfectly appropriate at the outset of an interview. It sets the tone.

4. When the pleasantries are over, she sits quietly and lets the interviewer take the lead, as is the employer's prerogative. There will be plenty of time for her to initiate later. Besides, the first five or ten minutes are critical, and Sally scrutinizes Edgar Employer with great care. She sizes him up, takes his measure, analyzes his personality, and second-guesses his background. She is aware that he is also sizing her up, deciding whether or not he likes her style, presence, appearance. She sits quietly, smiles responsively to his remarks, and tries to establish eye contact.

5. Sally has a strong but flexible personality. She instinctively adapts her personality to the style of the employer. If, for example, he appears stiff and formal, she will try to interject some humor. But the humor is appropriately subdued and formal. On the other hand, if

he is expansive and chatty, she makes certain that the conversation is not allowed to wander endlessly off into tangents without giving her a chance to sell herself a bit. Finally, if the interviewer seems ill at ease with a female professional, she tries to veer the conversation into substantive issues as soon as possible, figuring that this is the most neutral territory for an uptight man.

6. Sally is not a smoker, but even if she were, she'd be cautious about smoking in an office where the employer wasn't smoking. The presence of an ashtray is irrelevant. These days, nonsmokers are increasingly militant about their rights, and many openly prefer nonsmoking employees.

7. The absence of unpleasant mannerisms, physical and verbal, distinguishes Sally from other equally well-qualified applicants. Some people lace their sentences with "you know," "you have to understand," and so on. Others, especially when nervous, twirl their hair, stroke their beards, continually shift in their chairs, or gesticulate madly with their hands.

8. Sally knows that humor establishes immediate rapport, especially in awkward situations. It's not that she tries to be funny but rather that she remains good-humored. When the employer tries to make a joke or exchange a pleasantry, she shows she appreciates his attempt to warm things up a bit.

9. Sally is careful not to try to adopt a confessional tone with the employer, thus giving him the ammunition with which to shoot her. She doesn't, for example, apologize for what she doesn't have to offer: "Well, I know I don't have any experience, but. . . ."

10. Whatever her reservations about the job under discussion, she keeps her misgivings to herself. Once she receives an offer, there will be plenty of time to negotiate the specific terms. Until then, she must be positive—even downright enthusiastic—about the job.

11. Sally always conveys the impression that there are other irons in the fire, other choices. Above all, she is self-confident.

12. She is good at dealing with trick questions. Two of her favorites are, "Why should we hire you?" and "What is your major strength and weakness?" The first question tests grace under pressure; she tries to say something positive about herself as quickly as possible. With the latter query, she focuses on a strength that would be a big plus for this particular job and a weakness that would be irrelevant. She doesn't answer the question out of the context of the job interview. She would, for example, never tell the employer what she thinks her weakness as a person is. That's potentially more damaging than Edgar Employer has a right to know.

13. If the interview wanders into controversial issues, she knows how to assert herself sufficiently to work her way out of the bog. She keeps cool and tries to deal with the situation rationally rather than emotionally. If she can gracefully change the subject, she does so. Sometimes, she may even have to be blunt and say, "You know this is a fascinating but explosive topic. Can we talk more about your legal practice?"

14. At the close of the interview Sally thanks the interviewer and shakes hands.

After the Interview

Sally's thank-you note is succinct and well written, stating appreciation and/or pleasure in having met the interviewer: "Thank you for having taken the time to talk with me . . ."; interest in the job plus two or three reminders of her unique assets: "I feel certain that my experience as a _____ and my skills [or specific training] in _____ would enable me to make a positive contribution to your firm"; any other pertinent comment that will help.

Your Interview Savvy

Are you ready to test how good an interviewee you are? The following section deals with nine situations that commonly confront job applicants. Choose the best reply—A, B, or C. Then read the commentary to find out the strengths and weaknesses of each response. *Scoring:* 8–9 correct: Congratulations! 5–7 correct: Not bad; you are on the right track but must pay closer attention to the nuances of interviewing. Get more practice. 3–5 correct: There's hope, but reread the chapter; 0–3 correct: Further counseling is recommended.

1. *You arrive on time at the interview for the position of executive assistant to the company head but are kept waiting for twenty minutes. When the interview finally begins, the harassed employer, obviously hurrying to catch up on his schedule, asks you, "So why do you want to come and work for me?" Your answer: (A) "I don't really know. I thought you could tell me that." (B) "You obviously need someone to help relieve some of these time*

pressures you seem to be experiencing. I want to work for someone who needs an organized assistant. Apart from my formal academic training, I also have excellent time-management skills. I can help you to clear your desk for more important problems." (C) "Well, my degree in finance has trained me for a career in precisely the area you seem to be most concerned with these days, judging from that recent article about you in Fortune. Was it accurate at all?"

BEST ANSWER: A. _____   B. _____   C. _____

A has obviously failed to rise to the occasion. It is not the employer's job interview, but A's, and he should have attempted to say something specific and positive. B has tried to respond to the nuances of the man's difficult day, but his remarks are presumptuous and might possibly offend. Perhaps the employer thinks he's doing an excellent job of time management. C has a specific response to the actual question which shows that he also has done his homework in reading up on the firm in advance. Notice how he managed to get the conversational ball rolling by drawing the employer out with his own interesting question. He has made a good start.

2. *You are a second-year law student about to participate in your first on-campus interview at your school for a summer associate position in a law firm. You are also a forty-one-year-old former housewife who has never been employed as a professional before. The interviewer from a large urban corporate firm with a business practice asks kindly, "What made you choose law as a career?" (A) You answer, "I have always been fascinated by the legal*

process, especially as it affects the poor and the handicapped. For years I have worked as a key organizer in the League of Women Voters within the community, developed seminars on the disenfranchised, and published voter registration materials aimed specifically at minorities. However, since I have attended law school my interests have changed considerably. I now feel very strongly that tax law is my true calling." (B) You answer that because your former husband was a lawyer, you gained an exposure to law early on. When the time came to find yourself professionally, it was quite natural to apply to law school. (C) You answer that law is the kind of profession that provides security, money, and status. You feel that your values fit the position nicely.

BEST ANSWER: A _____   B _____   C _____

A has very nicely tried to bridge the gap between past and future. Notice how her answer reveals her serious professional commitment and avoids reference to her lack of experience, her age, or her marital status. Her personal problems have not intruded upon her answer. Notice also how she manages to swing her answer to tax law, a subject bound to interest a corporate firm more than her interest in the poor. B should not have referred to her lawyer husband. It may be of interest for the employer to know this, but not at the start of an interview before she has had a chance to create a positive professional image. C is also far too candid. Your professional motivation is weak if all you talk about are the benefits of the profession. It may be that many a successful lawyer has been motivated by similar desires, yet the answer is tactless and unprofessional.

3. *You are applying for a job as an urban planner at another state's planning commission, and you have traveled several hundred miles for the interview, which is held in a town of about 75,000. After a half-hour of conversation, the employer asks you, "Do you have any questions?" Your answer: (A) "Yes, do you consider my out-of-state background a handicap at all?" (B) "No, you seem to have covered everything quite thoroughly." (C) "Is there anything to do in this town after dark? Will I find it hard to get an apartment here?"*

BEST ANSWER: A ———   B ———   C ———

A has asked an appropriate and good question. Realizing that his outsider status might be a weakness, his object is to get the employer to talk it out so that he can get a chance to sell himself. B looks like a real "dodo." One should always have questions to ask. C shows his naivete in asking such questions before he has been offered the job. He is assuming too much, and his orientation is inappropriate. During the interview, he should be focusing on his professional assets rather than his personal concerns.

4. *You are preparing yourself for an accounting career, and this is your fifteenth on-campus interview with an accounting firm. You are the interviewer's twelfth appointment for that day, and you are allowed only twenty minutes to sell yourself. The employer looks at your résumé and then says, "Tell me about yourself, Miss Johnson." You respond (A) "Well, I was born in Vermont where I grew up on a farm. I was educated at Smith, where I majored in English. . . ." (B) "Well, there really isn't much to say that isn't repeated on that résumé you are*

holding. *What, in particular, did you want to know?" (C)
"Well, I think that my accounting experience last summer at Harvey & Billings has shown me what I can
contribute to a big eight accounting firm like yours. From
what I can gather, there seem to be few accountants with
my kind of specific legal background."*

BEST ANSWER: A _____ B _____ C _____

A has merely repeated autobiographical facts that the
interviewer can easily find on her résumé. She is wasting
everyone's time, and more importantly, she is boring. B
thinks that her résumé is more important than he is. She
is clearly shy, intimidated by the situation, and at a loss.
Her answer suggests that he resents having to talk and
is defensive. Notice her blunder in telling the interviewer to refer to her résumé. Clearly the interviewer's
question is directed at finding out what kind of a person
B is, and B's tactless and negative response has revealed
her weak interpersonal skills. C uses this small talk
opportunity to focus on her assets. Notice how
thoroughly she seems to have done her homework. She
understands the needs of the profession and can talk
quite specifically about her relevant strengths.

5. *You are twenty-three years old and a bright urban economics student, but you have never had any professional
work experience. The employer, a high-powered, middle-
aged economist, is interviewing you for a fine junior slot,
and the competition is stiff. He boldly asks, "Tell me, Mr.
Drozin, why should we hire you?" You reply (A) "Well,
I know I haven't had any real experience, but I think I
would do well." (B) "Gee, I really . . . well . . . let's see.
Frankly, I haven't thought about it. I am certain that*

*there are plenty of other equally well-trained candidates
around." (C) "I think that you should hire me because
I am extremely motivated to succeed as an economist,
and I will work very hard at the job."*

BEST ANSWER: A _____ B _____ C _____

A has made a fatal mistake of pointing out a negative
fact about himself to an interviewer. Never apologize for
what you cannot offer, and never give an employer a
reason to disqualify you. B has also made a fatal mistake: he is too modest about himself and can't think fast
enough on his feet. C obviously has a positive sense of
his own worth. He is not overwhelmed by his lack of
experience and won't allow the interviewer to focus on
it either. The employer's question is designed to test
whether or not he can think on his feet under pressure.
The specific content of the answer matters less than
answering it swiftly and positively.

6. *You are applying for a personnel spot in a large bank that
will require you to interview candidates for clerical positions. In the course of a leisurely and pleasant hour interview, the very poised employer asks, "Tell me, Ms. Gray,
what do you consider to be your chief weakness?" You say
(A) "Well, I think that I tend to be very impatient with
uneducated people who aren't on my intellectual level."
(B) "Well, I have always been very social and extrov-
erted. Sometimes I find myself wishing that I were more
inner-directed." (C) "I tend to be overly conscientious
about any responsibility I take on. I am a worry wart."*

BEST ANSWER: A _____ B _____ C _____

A has just blown her chances of getting the job because she has zeroed in on a weakness that makes her

unfit for the job. She should have chosen an irrelevant weakness. B is a shrewd young woman who realizes that her professed weakness is really a strength for an employee who must spend the day making small talk with job applicants. C wisely replies with an irrelevant weakness. Who cares if she is overly conscientious? Always pick a weakness that cannot be considered directly harmful to your job performance: that you are a stay-at-home, that you tend to spend too much money on clothes, that you watch too much television.

7. *A Ph.D. in History, you have decided to change careers and become a lawyer. At your very first interview for a summer associate job with a Wall Street firm, the middle-aged interviewer asks you this opening question, "Why did you decide to go to law school?" You answer (A) "Well, the job market dried up for history professors, and I decided upon law for a second career." (B) "Well, I have always wanted to become a lawyer, but my interest in history initially dominated because of a huge fellowship that I received and because of the opportunity to study with a renowned historian. If you are concerned that my Ph.D. will interfere with my success as a lawyer, I think that my grades and my law review experience suggest otherwise." (C) "I gather that your question is commonly asked of someone with my background. Do you find it a disturbing fact?"*

BEST ANSWER: A _____   B _____   C _____

This question is a killer. A does worst. He cites the facts—the poor job market—but does not make any positive statements about his motivation for a legal career. In fact, he doesn't answer the question at all. B is on a more positive track when he directly confronts the

supposed concern of the interviewer—the vague fear
that a Ph.D. in history will be less of a lawyer than
someone without it. Notice how he reminds the interviewer of his accomplishments in law school quite
gracefully. He makes himself seem a bright and successful person who has chosen between two good opportunities. He has avoided surrounding himself with a cloud
of failure; he has been consistently positive about himself. C's reply attempts to put the interviewer on the
defensive and get him to articulate what, precisely, it is
that bothers him about a former Ph.D. While it is not
a bad tactic for someone who otherwise might have been
prompted to say something negative about his decision,
his response does not give him the opportunity to be
positive about himself. And if the interviewer replies,
"No, it doesn't bother me at all," then C has lost the
opportunity to say something positive about his motiva-
tions for attending law school. This is unfortunate.

8. *You are applying for the second public relations job of
your professional career after having been fired from the
first job after nine months. You are twenty-four years old.
The interviewer asks you, "Why did you leave your last
job after such a short time?" (A) You reply that you did
not get along well with your boss, who was autocratic and
arbitrary. (B) You answer that you realized very quickly
that a huge organization was not the ideal starting point
for a young public relations person with a desire to do
many different jobs as fast as possible. You feel that the
hierarchial structure of the organization slowed you
down. Time was wasting away. (C) You say that you were
fired because you couldn't get along with your boss—a
man you intensely disliked.*

BEST ANSWER: A _____   B _____   C _____

If you have been fired from a job, never advertise it to an employer, especially if you technically "resigned." Your reasons may remain private or vague. One obvious exception is when your own situation is part of a larger layoff within an industry or organization. Then you are one among many, and you can afford to be quite open without stigmatizing yourself. A's response neatly avoids the bare facts but does focus in on the negatives of his situation. It would be better to be more positive. B's reply neatly avoids personalities in favor of more substantive aspects of the situation. The theory behind B's response is to avoid the hot potato completely. After all, an interview is not a confessional rite; you aren't obliged to tell an employer your private business. B's response leads very naturally into a discussion of why this new job, presumably with a smaller outfit, would be ideal. C has made the mistake of telling the unvarnished truth to someone who knows nothing about him and cannot properly put the incident into perspective.

9. *You are interviewing for a management job, and the employer asks mildly, "Where do you expect to be in ten years?" (A) You reply that you are unsure, but that you take solace in the fact that Peter Drucker has trouble with this hard question too! (B) You earnestly reply that in ten years you'd like to be an extremely successful professional within your field. (C) You reply that you do not know.*

BEST ANSWER: A _____   B _____   C _____

Many people find this an offensive or silly question, despite all the career-development materials that insist one must have a specific game plan for the future. To be sure, goals are critical for effective planning, but isn't five years good enough? A's answer tries to give some dash to his own expression of uncertainty. He makes it clear to the employer that he doesn't know but neither does an expert. Fair enough. His reply is self-confident, which is always important. B gives a vague answer that may prompt further questioning. C's response does not measure up at all. His answer does not challenge the query, as did A's response. Instead he drops the ball completely. His vagueness will undoubtedly disturb an employer.

Now that you are well prepared for your interviews, polish and practice your skills so that you can sail through this final, crucial phase with complete self-assurance. Good luck in choosing among the enticing job offers that are about to come your way.

6

Strategies for Success on the Job

Congratulations! You've worked hard to get the job you want and can now look forward to an exciting career. Armed with your degree, skills, and enthusiasm, you already have many of the ingredients for career success. But just as you planned earlier for success in the job search, so you must now prepare for success on the job. A smooth transition from student life to the professional world may require a far greater adjustment of attitude, style, and performance than you expect. But the stress of adapting to a very different milieu should be more than offset by the sense of pride you will soon feel in your own personal growth.

For example, let's look at the critical issue of how success is measured. During college or graduate school, your abilities were measured primarily by the *objective* standards of test scores and/or term papers. So, if a particular professor may have found you too quiet or in some way difficult to reach, no matter; his subjective evaluation of you was unlikely to affect your grade adversely. Thus it is possible to achieve academic "success" without the complicating factor of subjective and interpersonal issues. Moreover, the fact that as a student you could generally work at your own pace, wear the clothes of your choice, and *select* courses, college majors, and even term paper topics signifies a lifestyle of unusual autonomy, independence, and control.

As a worker, the situation will be different. You will take direction from others and typically have little or no say about the tasks on which you focus your daily efforts. Autonomy will probably be slight. Moreover, just as "chemistry" counted in the employer's decision to hire you, when you're on the job it will also count in your "success." How others feel about working with you will probably matter as much, if not more, than the quality of the actual work you do.

Regardless of your intellectual horsepower and ability to achieve results, others will expect you to be pleasant, cooperative, and reliable. Indeed, the ability to get along with people and to "fit in" to the specific work environment will be related to the employer's perception of your competence. Every major study of career failure among "high-fliers" or fast-trackers emphasizes that for all their brilliance, they were eventually "derailed"—to cite a term used by the Atlanta-based Center for Creative Leadership—if they were arrogant or insensitive to others.

What follows is a practical guide to performing well on the job—in all its aspects. This chapter will provide practical suggestions that will demystify the new and often confusing ground rules of the working world. It will also provide guidelines that you need in order to develop into a mature professional, at the same time avoiding the typical pitfalls.

Understanding the Ground Rules

Understanding "Professionalism"

Janet Murphy was the kind of bright, self-confident, and articulate bank trainee that everyone in personnel predicted would rise fast on the management track. However, after two weeks on her first full-time job, she had alienated the president's secretary with her "snippiness," openly called a particular task "boring," gossiped about a fellow trainee, and turned in a memorandum full of grammatical and typographical errors. Her boss pointed out that her behavior was childish and "unprofessional." Janet was smart enough to set about rescuing herself from a bad start.

What does it mean to behave like a professional? In popular usage, "professional" describes an exceptionally motivated person who lives up to the highest standards of his/her occupational field. In the past, the word meant membership in a high-status occupational group such as law or medicine. Today, the word is so widely used that a person can be a "pro" in any career field.

What characterizes a pro? First and foremost, the commitment to do a superb job and to do it the right way. In addition, when the pressure is on, the true professional keeps cool, motivates others, and proceeds to solve the problem or complete the task logically and effectively. It is the pro's characteristic dedication that results in personal plans getting cancelled if a crisis brews.

The pro has a positive manner and keeps emotions firmly in check. For example, if you were to show up very late for an appointment with a pro, you would not be made aware of any irritation since the pro doesn't waste energy getting upset or expressing negative *personal* feelings. In contrast, if the same incident were to happen with a novice, you'd likely be made aware of your *faux pas.*

As a professional you have a new role to play just as you play other roles as a student, friend, son, or daughter. While you have had experience with these other roles (i.e., being thoughtful enough to buy Mother's Day cards, caring enough to listen to friends' problems, etc.), you will need to learn the special requirements and expected behaviors of the role of a professional. Some of these, such as finishing work quickly, may be habitual with you. But other behaviors, such as keeping your feelings in check, may not. The specific topics discussed in the following pages will help you to learn what is expected.

Maintaining a Professional Image

A professional "image" includes your choice of wardrobe, grooming, and various elements of body language such as posture and hand gestures. By now, as most new professionals realize, image—although it relates to surface matters—has a lot to do with having your overall performance taken seriously and accorded respect. Now that you are a full-fledged worker, you're no longer dressing just for yourself. At the outset, the way you dress is important. Ultimately, once you are past the first-impressions stage, achievement, teamwork, or good relations with fellow employees will be more important criteria.

What does this mean in terms of wardrobe? High-quality

clothes that are moderately conservative will stand you in good stead. Several good-fitting suits (and/or dresses) well accessorized are always a good choice. A neutral trenchcoat can act as topcoat and raincoat. If money is a problem, and it often is for new professionals, your most substantial investment might be your shoes and other leather goods.

Women have an additional consideration. They must balance the desire to look feminine with the need to appear absolutely professional. Cultivating an image that calls too much attention to the feminine may be distracting, but a "sexless" professional look is not the answer either. Women who work in a predominantly male environment must strike some sort of balance they can live with, one that seems appropriate to the office atmosphere. If there's any doubt that dangling earrings, heavy makeup, or strong perfume might confuse your best efforts, opt for a more conservative look.

Even if co-workers at your level dress casually, it might be to your advantage to concentrate on the kind of neat, professional appearance associated with the *next job* up the ladder (as long as that does not make you look as though you're competing with your boss). You want people to conclude you can reach that next rung easily. Interestingly, others will "read" self-assurance (or lack of it) into the image you project.

Grooming is equally important. Needless to say, your personal hygiene should be above reproach. Shoes should always be polished and in good condition (i.e., attending to run-down heels before they're apparent); and clothes should fit properly, neither too loose nor too tight.

Your nonverbal language also says a great deal about you to others. If your college placement office has a videotape facility where you can see your behavior on tape, by all means take advantage of it to arrange a mock interview. When you actually see some of your mannerisms, such as hair twirling, finger tapping, or a slouching posture, you'll probably feel uneasy; but the experience will help you to make needed changes.

Now let's turn to more substantive aspects of what is meant by professionalism.

Performance on the Job

Since first impressions do count, from the very beginning do the best job you can, whether the task is trivial, such as photocopying, or substantive, such as writing a memorandum. Since you must expect to be "tested" by your boss with a variety of assignments, don't rank the tasks. Do *everything* well.

There are several nuts-and-bolts dimensions to performance, a few of which are listed here:

1. *Speed.* While rushing through work is pointless, people do like quick (and excellent) results. Take the time to do a good job, but be sensitive to turning in a memorandum or report *sooner* rather than later. If your work is done well and quickly, others will take notice.

2. *Deadlines.* Your ability to meet deadlines is critical. Many studies, such as one from the American Management Association, have shown how highly most managers value dependability in subordinates. Your manager won't be pleased if only a portion of your work is delivered on time, since any missed deadlines on your part jeopardize his ability to meet deadlines farther up the line.

Be realistic about the time you'll need to get a job done

before you promise it for a specific date. Avoid being heroic in aspiration and disappointing in result. If you realize that you can't meet the appointed deadline, say so at the earliest opportunity. Bosses don't like surprises. Having to apologize for a missed deadline is far worse than giving an early warning of trouble, when additional help might be enlisted or priorities reordered.

3. *Punctuality.* In a sense, being punctual is a form of meeting a deadline. If you are late, neither excuses nor self-justifications are likely to help your cause.

Note too that in some organizations, even if you stay until 8:30 every night, you still are expected to arrive at 8:00 A.M. or at least at the same time (or before) your boss. For some recent graduates, this issue of earning "brownie points" is hard to understand because neither time nor punctuality— let alone brownie points—may have previously mattered in achieving good results. However silly it seems, in most companies you'll need to manage appearances as carefully as you manage results. In the work culture, being at work on time or working "regular" hours enables everyone else around to see you making an effort at your job!

Asking Necessary Questions, and Other Work Habits

Asking questions is part and parcel of being a new employee; feeling any embarrassment about it is a waste of energy. When given an assignment, you need to clarify what's expected of you before risking mistakes. This is often easier said than done, since not all managers give clear or sufficiently comprehensive guidelines. However, it is more important for you to do the job right than to worry if others will think less of you for seeking clarification. The chances are that your manager will be glad to elaborate or clear up confusion.

Similarly, if someone is explaining a complicated procedure, don't expect perfect recall. Take notes if that's the best way for you. Don't fall into the typical newcomer trap of wanting to "look smart" or have your results seem effortless.

The Importance of Completed Work

While it would be nice if others were willing to tolerate your rough drafts, that's an unrealistic expectation. Any work will now be judged as "final." So if you are asked to prepare a letter for your manager, write the very best possible letter and have it typed on the company letterhead with only a signature necessary to complete it. Whatever other kinds of assignments you receive, complete the task to the most logical final stage. Learn to present neat, appealing, and finished-looking work at all times.

In sending memos to your boss, find out what is expected. Does everyone submit only perfectly typed one-pagers or are neatly handwritten notes often sufficient? Learning what's expected can save time and effort. Ask your colleagues (or your boss) to show you good memos and reports prepared by someone at your level.

Communicating Succinctly

Being a succinct communicator will earn you high marks with others, since this is a prized skill. Train yourself to organize your thoughts in advance so you can speak more concisely. Don't take seven sentences to explain a problem when one sentence would do, followed by a brief presentation of a *solution* (if possible). If you operate on the assumption that no one will want to listen to you for more than one minute, you'll be on safe ground. Besides, if they are sufficiently interested in what you have to say, they can always ask for more detail.

Your co-workers will also prefer an organized colleague. Feel free to ask questions, but avoid "overcommunicating." One phone call to cover three requests is better than three successive calls of one brief request each.

Avoid unnecessary drop-in visits to gossip or pass the time. Unless you restrict socializing to lunchtime or after hours, word will get around that you aren't a "good worker" or worse, that you interfere with the productivity of others. Even if you turn out to be a conspicuously hard worker who just likes to socialize a bit from 9:00 to 9:30 every day, remember, you are at work to work, not to play. While everyone needs to take a breather, keep your own meanderings on the moderate side.

The Team Player

Depending upon your sense of independence, it may be difficult for you to seek help from others when you are given a complex project to do. When you were a student, typically you were on your own.

Now you'll find that people are highly interdependent: few performers can complete their work solely on their own. Chances are, whatever your job, you'll need the help of others to achieve your goals. And as a good team player, you'll help others to achieve their goals as well. If you learn to think and talk "we" instead of "I," you'll be cued to valuable team lingo. Be alert to how important the team approach is at your organization.

Polishing Presentation Skills

Before attending meetings, you will need to do homework. Anticipate possible questions or requests for information that your boss may make. Have copies of key documents or files with you. If others will attend, find out what other materials you'll need to bring.

In any group discussion, people are vulnerable, so make sure your comments advance your cause. Even if your remarks are generally cogent, be sensitive to the overall amount of time you take. Strive for moderation in the frequency of your comments. And heated debate—even if you were the campus debating champion—is unwise. On a new job, it's best to be an observer in any group setting until you learn the cast of players or their relationships and rivalries. Understand your environment before you seek too much exposure; keep a low profile at first.

Also keep in mind that if you are with senior people, an ill-considered or shallow remark at a meeting can create a lasting first impression. Since you only have one chance to make that first impression, use it well, especially in meetings. When you are with senior people, keep your remarks concise. The higher up you go in the organization, the more time is equated with money.

Understanding Office Customs

Every office has its own style and culture. But there are some general truths:

Personal calls. If Sally Smith works ten hours a day, does she have the right to make personal phone calls at work? Not really. It may not seem fair, but new employees must refrain from too much personal telephone time. If you need to make a personal call, be discreet about it, and keep the call brief. If you can, make personal calls first thing in the morning, during lunch, or after 5:00 P.M. While all workers have to make such calls occasionally, conducting the business of your personal life at the office can be damaging to your professional image. Keep the two worlds separate.

Neatness. Keep a neat and tidy desk. Let others see you as in control of your clutter. Avoid a sloppy office atmosphere such as shoes under the desk or personal belongings strewn around.

Manners. Good manners—being polite, saying thank you, writing a courteous note of thanks after someone has done you a favor—are the niceties that make life more pleasant and ease work relationships.

Be sensitive to your colleagues' habits and preferences. Smokers sharing offices with nonsmokers should be considerate. If office quarters are close, keep your telephone voice modulated, and limit your use of scent to a light cologne or aftershave. While a jar of jelly beans on your desk may help you to break the ice with others, small breaches of courtesy, such as "borrowing" scissors without permission (and then forgetting to return them), may freeze things up.

A cheerful, positive, and even-keeled demeanor is also important. Others like to know what to expect when they work closely with you, and moody people have an unsettling effect on morale. And remember, no matter how justified anger may be, open conflicts are not only disruptive but potentially damaging. Think twice before you blow up at someone in the hope that "clearing the air" will be good for both of you. Better to cool off and resolve differences at another time.

Profiting from Feedback

A good way to succeed at the job is to seek an early reading of how others feel about you, so you can make whatever adjustments and changes seem in order. Many otherwise motivated employees fail to solicit reactions from colleagues and superiors, since it's only human to avoid hearing about imperfections. At the same time bosses may be reluctant to criticize, hoping that the situation will improve. However, as a newcomer, it's doubly important to question your manager directly about areas where your performance could stand improvement.

Typically, of course, what you hear may be criticism rather than praise. If your boss responds: "I've noticed that you often come in late," to your questionning, don't be defensive or try to justify yourself. "Well, I've had a lot of trouble with my travel connections," is a less preferable response than simply saying, "I've had some problems and I'm working on them; I'll try to improve."

Every few months you might continue to ask how you are doing.

Showing Initiative

Acting rather than reacting is one of the keys to getting ahead. Your capacity for taking the initiative can be demonstrated in a number of ways. You might:

1. Introduce yourself to key people in your department rather than waiting to be introduced if sufficient time has elapsed and you still have not meet these people.

2. Learn the names and functions of senior people in all relevant departments of the organization so you'll know who they are when you do meet them.

3. Volunteer for extra work when you see a job that needs to be done. Straightening the files is one possibility. Others will present themselves if you're alert.

4. Demonstrate your interest in the details of the company. A bright newcomer in one organization spotted an advertisement for a new product with the exact name as one that was under active consideration at her own company. By alerting the New Products Manager to the outside ad, she helped the company save valuable time, and avoided a possible trademark problem.

The combination of hard work and initiative will be seen as a sign of your commitment and loyalty to the new job. The more you show that you are willing to cooperate and give of yourself, the more others will count on you and consider you responsible. A willingness to be flexible about time is important as well. While in many organizations there is a large contingent of "nine-to-fivers," don't be eager to be out of the building at "official" closing time.

Relationships and the Power Structure

Since many, if not most, hierarchical organizations are modeled on the military, the chain of command concept dominates. (Betty L. Harragan's book, *Games Your Mother Never Taught You,* is an enlightening introduction to such organizations.)

One important link in the chain-of-command structure is loyalty. Never "bad mouth" your company to outsiders. Be careful what you say to co-workers who may later quote you. For example, confiding to a co-worker, "I've come to this organization to bolster my credentials. After that I'll move on to something more exciting" is the sort of damaging (even if true) statement that might easily be passed along. Similarly, when you hear several co-workers complaining about someone, you'd be well-advised to be a quiet listener rather than an outspoken critic. You never know when a company reorganization may turn you into that person's colleague, boss, or subordinate. Alliances and relationships formed at work can shift quickly.

A good general rule is to refrain from making critical remarks about your boss to *anyone* in the company. If there is a serious conflict between the two of you, try to straighten it out directly. Never go to a higher level no matter how justified you may feel. The same goes for putting any criticism in writing; the written word can have a rather stinging permanence.

Your Relationship with Your Boss

If your organization has a hierarchical structure, as do most, satisfying your boss is a high priority. After all, your boss is the person who will evaluate your performance, champion your potential to others, and push through your merit raises. He or she becomes the authority on the subject of you and your performance.

"Managing up" is a term used widely to describe the

delicate challenge of getting along with your boss. For example, how does your boss like to learn about new information—by reading a memo or by hearing about it face to face? As Peter Drucker, the eminent author of numerous books on management, suggests, if you have an idea you wish to present to your boss, do so in the style he prefers. In addition, find out if your boss prefers that employees make an appointment for a discussion or whether drop-in visits are acceptable. When is your boss most accessible—at lunch, after 5:00, or before 9:00? Does he seem particularly interested in training and developing his staff? (If not, expect to depend on your own initiative.) No matter what, keep in mind that your dependability, loyalty, and capacity to follow instructions intelligently will strongly influence the trust and respect your boss feels for you.

Relationships with Your Colleagues

Whereas the power balance with your boss is obvious, power also plays a role in your relationships with your colleagues. As a team player interested in building successful alliances, you'll need to be both a giver and an influencer. Mastering techniques of give and take and persuasion will be the challenge. For example, if you are up to your ears in work and a colleague asks you to read a draft memo, find the time to do so even if you have to take the work home. Saying no at such a time could weaken your relationship, and very likely there will come a time when you want the favor returned. If you do have to say no, say it diplomatically (i.e., "I'd love to do it, but unfortunately the X project is due tomorrow, and I can't give you my reaction until after that. Would that be okay?"). Soften that "no" so it is a qualified, rather than a direct negative.

Relationships with Influential Others

When you are a new employee, it may be difficult to identify the people of most possible help to you. For example, a secretary who has been with the company 20 years and is a pal of the president's wife may be a goldmine for important company background information. A friend of your boss down the hall from you who can observe your comings and goings can form a positive impression of you that can count heavily. Many people, whether you realize it or not, can open doors for you. And impressions are often based more upon an assessment of your interpersonal skills than your actual work performance.

When you don't know "who's who," the best plan is to take on any job you're asked to do, and do it as well as you can. Assume you wouldn't be asked unless that person had the right to do so. If you're hesitant, temporize by saying, "I'd be delighted to do it for you, but do you mind if I check first with my boss to see if there's anything else that comes first?" Otherwise, you can seem uncooperative when, in fact, you are simply not sure of what's expected of you.

Keep in mind that when you're new in an organization, you're in a fishbowl.

Coping with the Organizational Battlefield

Every new professional comes up against company politics. In some organizations, the game of politics is rampant and distasteful. In most others, however, being "political" means little more than mingling freely and forging alliances easily. Generally, it also means maintaining a professionally friendly relationship with a person regardless of your subjective feelings. While nearly everyone has dislike for the person who becomes the smooth but hypocritical "politician," it is wise always to be diplomatic, but not too chummy until you know your way through the minefields.

In reality, while some colleagues may seem cooperative and friendly, they can still be quiet (or not-so-quiet) competitors. So be especially careful about confidences that may turn out to be damaging self-disclosures. You'll need also to develop your own point of view about where you stand on the issues of competition and cooperation. Clearly the competitive element is reduced in a high-growth organization where opportunities for promotion abound. But in others, where the pyramidal structure or sluggish profits leave little room at the top, fierce competition is likely. Nonetheless, success in such an environment still requires a good measure of cooperation, team behavior, and leadership. There are always some people who manage to achieve great work results without hurting others or acting aggressively toward their peers. They earn the respect of others and will serve as useful role models for you.

Understanding the Culture

"Culture," a word much bandied about, refers to the unspoken rules of an organization. In some organizations, being a team player is vital. In others, being individually creative is considered important.

How do you discover the culture of your organization? The best way is by interviewing a longtime employee who is willing to be candid. Ask him or her, "What kind of traits do people value?" Or "What makes for success in this organization?" "Are there any taboos?"

From the start, you should understand that professional

relationships, for the most part, are different from personal relationships. Many graduates begin in a new job hoping to build a cadre of friends. And they're quite right—friends are often a natural result of the work situation. But they often confuse the relationship with the role. Being professional is getting the job done, and understanding that personal relationships must sometimes take a secondary position. If your best friend gets into work difficulty because of a serious blunder, your loyalties can easily be divided. Suppose the company is compromised or the success of a major team project wrecked? It won't be easy to combine the sympathy of a friend with the objectivity of a professional, but it's something you will need to learn.

Communication Style

In the work world, people are rarely terminated for lack of competence; they're terminated for personality clashes, or for a lack of "fit" that translates into a matter of "style" or "chemistry." Understanding that there are significant stylistic differences among people will make it easier for you to adapt to others and communicate smoothly.

Drake Beam Morin, Inc., has developed an instrument called "I-Speak" that uses and simplifies a theory about communication style developed by the Swiss psychologist Carl Jung. The "I-Speak" identifies four communication styles: feeler, thinker, sensor, and intuitor. Let's look at these.

The feeler is oriented toward people and tends to interpret data and events in terms of their likely impact upon people or his own feelings. For example, if a feeler is told about a necessary staff cutback, his first question will likely be, "How will people feel about these cuts?" Feelers are "people" persons who often mistake their emotional reactions for actual reality or facts. For example, if a feeler is upset about staff cuts, he assumes that everyone else is too.

The thinker is unusually systematic. He weighs the pros and cons of a situation and seeks as many facts as possible before making a decision. Thinkers are often strategic planners or long-range evaluators, better at making sound judgments than getting things done efficiently or following through on details.

The sensor is a results-oriented do-it-now type of person. "Don't tell me how you feel, or the pros and cons of it; just get it done," the sensor might say. Business executives who are sensors are often very decisive, but they may need to slow down and weigh decisions more carefully if they are to get the best possible results.

The intuitor is a creative visionary type who is concerned with concepts, the future or the "big" picture. But for all his artistic or intellectual brilliance, he often will have trouble dealing with the boring little details necessary to get a task done.

According to Jung, we are each a combination of all four types, although one type tends to predominate. What type are you? What type do you think your boss is? Knowledge of your communication style and that of others will enable you to modify your own style or become more flexible. A clash in styles often biases people against the actual merit of whatever may be proposed. For example, if you are a sensor, or action-oriented person, you may feel impatient with a feeler's seemingly endless small talk aimed at getting to know you. Regardless, you'll need to modify that impatience if you want to succeed in influencing the person. (The "I-Speak" instrument is incorporated along with extensive application exercises into Career Navigator Ⓣ: The Computer-Powered Job Search System, published by Drake Beam Morin, Inc., in New York.)

How Your Present Job Relates to Your Future

Your present job offers an excellent opportunity to develop new skills or to use skills you most enjoy. While it's important to plan for the future, focus on performance in your present job. If you can integrate your specific career goals into actual work tasks that also mesh with the company's strategic objectives, that is ideal. But it is far more likely to happen if you take the initiative for developing your own concrete career objectives as well as an action plan to reach them.

Don't be the kind of person who always seems to be concerned about future awards and promotions. Live in the present; it's the most effective and enjoyable approach to your career. To be perceived as someone who's always asking for things and who is never satisfied until he gets this promotion or that raise, will mark you as unduly ambitious or neurotic.

Remember, those who are in a position to influence your career are often basing their judgment about you on mere fragments of information. A person who is two levels higher than your boss may come to conclusions about you based on ten minutes in a meeting. Unfair as it is, that is the reality. So manage such opportunities as appropriately as you can to develop your skills and knowledge and bring them to the attention of those who can further your career.

Discuss the topics in this chapter with good friends who are also starting their professional lives. This kind of important give-and-take will give you an idea of other organizations, their "culture," and how best to attain your own possible career satisfaction.

Index